LONDON TRANSPORT
in the 1920s

Michael H. C. Baker

Ian Allan PUBLISHING

Contents

Introduction	... ...	3
1.	Setting the Scene	6
2.	The Tube — Replacing the Originals	20
3.	The Surface Lines	32
4.	Whither the Tram?	42
5.	Bus Scene 1920	54
6.	Think of a Number	64
7.	The General Strike	70
8.	Big Building Projects	74
9.	The Modern Bus	80
10.	Towards the Country and a New Decade... ...	86
Bibliography	... ...	96

Picture credits
All photographs are from the author's collection, except where individually credited.

First published 2009

ISBN 978 0 7110 3367 2

All rights reserved. No part of this book may be reproduced or transmitted in any form or by any means, electronic or mechanical, including photocopying, recording or by any information storage and retrieval system, without permission from the Publisher in writing.

© Michael H. C. Baker 2009

Published by Ian Allan Publishing

an imprint of Ian Allan Publishing Ltd, Hersham, Surrey, KT12 4RG

Printed in England by Ian Allan Printing Ltd, Hersham, Surrey, KT12 4RG

Code: 0905/B

Visit the Ian Allan Publishing website at www.ianallanpublishing.com

EDE

Introduction

THERE has probably never been a decade when public transport made such progress as the 1920s. This was the first decade without horse-drawn buses or trams in the capital. Electrification had arrived on the underground railways as well as the street tramways some 20 years earlier, and on the lines which in 1933 would become part of London Transport it was only way out in the Home Counties, where Middlesex met Buckinghamshire, that steam power still prevailed, although on the main lines steam would last until the 1960s. South of the Thames electrification on the surface suburban lines belonging to the Southern Railway, created in 1923 by an amalgamation of the South Eastern & Chatham, the London, Brighton & South

The author's father, awaiting demobilisation near the Suez Canal early in 1919.

Coast and the London & South Western railways, proceeded apace. It was a different story north of the Thames, for although there was some electrification on the main-line railways it was the Underground group which was the driving force.

To begin at the beginning. As a new decade dawned on 1 January 1920 it was the fervent wish of the population of London and the Home Counties that the horrors of the previous one be left behind. This was hardly possible for many who had lost family and friends; their lives would be forever changed. Some 25 years later, although such would not have occurred to a seven-year-old, many of my primary-school teachers were unmarried ('spinsters' was the term used), because the young men to whom they had been — or to whom they hoped to be — engaged had not come back from the war. Although World War 1 had ended at 11am on 11 November 1918 some conscripts had found themselves still occupied in fighting in Ireland, Russia and the Middle East; at the beginning of 1920 125,000 were still awaiting demobilisation.

It seems largely to have escaped the notice of historians that this resulted in a number of mutinies. Men with industrial skills, which included London General Omnibus Co (LGOC) mechanics and drivers, were demobbed first — nearly two thirds of LGOC drivers and conductors served in the war — but as many of these had only fairly recently been called up it caused much unrest amongst others. In Epsom, for instance, a group of Canadian soldiers, frustrated at the lack of a ship to take them home, rioted, broke into the police station and killed a policeman. My father, a driver with the British Mediterranean Expeditionary Force, was involved in a mutiny early in 1919. Along with thousands of others he was based near Cairo, awaiting a ship home, and each night patrols would be sent out to keep peace in the city. Every so often a pot-shot would be taken at these patrols, sometimes with fatal consequences. Having survived some five years of war the troops decided that enough was enough, and

3

one evening it was agreed that all would refuse to go out. Dad, a corporal, said that the junior officers were aware of this and gave the men's action tacit approval. Within days a ship arrived, and the entire camp marched aboard. Upon arrival at Southampton the troops were paraded on the quayside, where they were addressed by a general who told them they would be immediately 'demobbed', and that not a word of what had taken place was to be breathed, even to their families. This they must have accepted, for although Dad regularly attended regimental reunions it was not until almost the last, in the early 1960s, that he told me the story.

The great fear amongst the Establishment, looking apprehensively towards Russia and Germany, was Communism — or, as it was often termed, Bolshevism. In 1920 ex-servicemen marched on Downing Street, calling for a better deal, whilst army chiefs were working on plans 'in the event of a Soviet government being set up in Liverpool'. Many ex-servicemen faced unemployment, there was much industrial unrest, and in 1919 some 2.4 million British workers were involved in some form of strike action, resulting in the loss of 35 million working days. In 1922 the British Legion estimated that there were one million ex-servicemen without jobs. It is hardly surprising that 1926 saw Britain's one and only General Strike — of which more anon.

The class system, threatened by left-wing agitation coupled with a disillusionment with those in power who had taken the country into the horrors of the 1914-18 war, nevertheless remained remarkably resilient. Public transport was for the middle class and, to a lesser extent, the working class, although a large proportion of the latter continued to walk or cycle to work. The more staid members of the upper classes owned limousines, the younger ones fast sports cars. Bertie Wooster, when not dashing up to town by the Great Western Railway or in an Alvis or a Bentley, travelled around it in a taxi. The story goes that a member of the aristocracy, thinking that he ought to sample a ride in an omnibus, climbed aboard and said to the conductor: "No 11 Cadogan Square, my good man!" My mother, one of those who had lost their father in the war, and who was a maid to just such a family in their London home off Sloane Square, said it was probably true. Yet the omnibus, a familiar sight in the West End, *was* helping to make the world more egalitarian — much more so than the tram, which generally kept itself to the East End and the suburbs. Young women, regardless of class, the bolder ones no longer concerned whether or not they revealed their ankles (or, indeed, their knees), happily climbed to the upper deck and took delight in viewing London from on high. Gustav Holst wrote music in the bus on his way to teach the girls of St Paul's School, Hammersmith;

Above: One wonders if the irony of the poster immediately above his head was apparent to the driver of this MET 'A'-type tram of 1904/5, photographed at Wood Green in the winter of 1929/30. At the best of times there could be fewer colder jobs in the public-transport world than standing at the controls of a tram, lacking any sort of protection above the waist, in all sorts of weather; the winter of 1929/30 was particularly bad.

Above right: Ludgate Circus in the early 1920s. B72 (LN 4772) in the foreground, another heading towards St Paul's and taxis with folding hoods mingle with horse- and errand-boy-propelled transport. All the men — civilians and a soldier and a sailor — wear hats. Today the railway bridge supporting the line connecting Blackfriars and the South London railway network with the Underground and North London has been replaced by a tunnel, but route 6 still terminates at Kensal Rise, although its eastern terminus is now the Aldwych.

Right: Traffic aplenty in Victoria Street, looking west. One wonders at what point the gentleman in the white coat realised that erecting a ladder in the middle of a bus queue was not a terribly good idea. The not-very-helpful original caption gives the date as 1920-30, but we can narrow it down to sometime in the middle of the period, for there are NSs as well as Bs, Ks and Ss, and none has pneumatic tyres.

John Betjeman, beginning the journey which would see him established as the most popular English poet of the century, constantly featured in his work trips in and around London by bus, electric train, tram, and, later, trolleybus, whilst the red London bus cropped up again and again in the paintings of the Camden Town Group, which included Sickert, Ginner, Spencer Gore, Bevan and Nevinson, among others.

Michael H. C. Baker
Wareham
January 2009

· 1 ·

Setting the Scene

BY THE beginning of 1920 most conscripts were back in civilian life with the equivalent of 26 weeks' wages whilst they looked for work. After I completed National Service in January 1958 my employer of two years previously had to take me back. There was no such guarantee after World War 1. However, the London General Omnibus Co, the Tramways Department of the London County Council, the Underground and other tram and bus companies operating in and around the capital usually took back returning military personnel, just as the B-type buses that had been commandeered (and had survived) returned to work for the LGOC. Nearly two thirds of the LGOC's employees had taken part in the war, but not all who survived it returned unharmed. At meeting of the Directors on 24 July 1919 it was noted that 'a total of 773 cases of disabled soldiers and sailors have been reported to the TQT Mutual Aid Fund and submitted particulars as to the manner in which the cases have been dealt with'.

Remembrance Sunday (1 November) 1923.
LGOC bus men, all wearing medals from service in World War 1, accompanied by another WW1 veteran, B23 'Ole Bill', parade past the Cenotaph in Whitehall.

Left: King George V shaking hands with busmen, all ex-servicemen, from Middle Row garage, Kensington, at Buckingham Palace, 14 February 1920.

Below: One of the most fascinating pictures in the London Transport Museum collection. A line of 12 LGOC B-type double-deckers belonging to the private-hire department, led by B4895 and preceded by charabanc XF 8008, prepare to set off on a children's outing organised by Dalston garage, August 1926.
A lone policeman has little to do apart from providing a presence, although he'll probably tell the children sitting on the side of the charabanc to resume their seats, as parents, older brothers and sisters, busmen and others stand and chat. It is not quite possible to read what is written on the clown's costume other than the initials L.G.O.C. (the official General clown?), but the picture provides us with a fascinating glimpse of the organisation that would have gone into providing a day out for East End children, many of them no doubt with a father out of work or, worse, killed in the war.
London Transport Museum

But the return of former soldiers meant that their replacements were no longer needed. At a Board meeting on 4 March 1920 it was recorded that 'it has been necessary to dismiss 500 Drivers and Conductors owing to the return of further employees from War Service, and to the reduction in the number of 'Buses operating. The Men's Union was taking serious exception to the numbers of dismissals and was threatening trouble. The Chairman stated that while the Company's action was perfectly reasonable, it might be desirable, as a matter of policy, to compromise in some way.' This was agreed to. A job on the buses, trams or Underground railways was highly valued, and employees — and, indeed, their families — were generally well treated. Pensions, at that time very much the exception rather than the rule for most workers, were paid by the LGOC. In November 1920 the Board agreed to pay 'a pension of eleven shillings per week to Ex Conductor E. Harding, aged 59 with 40 years' service, discharged on account of ill health'.

Some young men, having acquired skills in a war which was described as the first truly mechanical one, bought a war-surplus bus or lorry — or, quite often,

a vehicle that could be used as either —and set up in business. A downpayment of £100 was all that was necessary; the Metropolitan Police had to approve the roadworthiness of the vehicle, but, that done, it could operate wherever its owner chose. This initially had little effect on established services in the capital, rather more out in the suburbs and beyond. At the beginning of 1920 the demand for buses far out-stripped the number available, and there was plenty of scope for those who were prepared to take up the challenge. Very few of these enterprises were long-lived, but a few flourished and would cause con-siderable anxiety to 'the General' and other members of the Underground Group — the Combine. The very first 'pirate' bus to operate in Central London began work on route 11, perhaps London's most famous, on 5 August 1922, and by the end of 1923 there were 70 such operators. Meanwhile the LGOC, drastically short of vehicles, was introducing new buses as fast as AEC could build them. On 7 October 1920 the directors authorised the purchase of no fewer than 1,000 K types and 265 of the more advanced Ss. The pirates' favourite types were the Leyland LB and the Dennis London, both of normal-control layout, *i.e.* with the driver sitting behind the engine, unlike the forward-control Ks and Ss.

The bus companies were competing not only amongst themselves but also with the trams, and the latter began to suffer. Although the tram would not finally disappear from the streets of London until

Above: A 'pirate' bus, LH 8790 of the Allen company. From the earliest days London buses have advertised films. Although now largely forgotten, Laurette Taylor, born in New York in 1884, was a significant actress of the period, and *Peg O' My Heart*, written by her second husband, the splendidly named J. Hartley Manners, was one of the smash hits of 1922. Noel Coward wrote *Hay Fever* (1925) after spending a weekend at her home, and although she later became a victim of alcoholism she continued to act almost until her death in 1946; the previous year she had starred in *The Glass Menagerie* by Tennessee Williams, who spoke of 'a radiance about her art'. Ah, the bus. Well, not a lot we can tell you. The Allen company is not mentioned in Brewster's *London Independent Bus Operators 1922-1933*, although the address of proprietor William Percy Allen — 64-70 Vauxhall Bridge Road — is clear enough on the body side. The bodywork does not resemble any I have seen portrayed, and, as for the chassis, the absence of vents on the bonnet side is most unusual and does not conform with contemporary Leyland or Dennis practice.

1952 (and would reappear nearly 50 years later) there were those who by the early 1920s foresaw its demise. From the outset the London County Council had operated its trams under two huge handicaps. One was that it was largely prevented from penetrating the heart of the West End and the City of London, the second that where it did manage this and in the inner suburbs it was forced to use the highly expensive and troublesome conduit system. Maintenance of the

Above: Three rather jolly 'pirates' pose beside L61 (XR 6498), a Leyland LB of Veleta, at Myatt's Park, Camberwell, on a Sunday morning *c*1925.

Below: A cyclist pedals past a 'pirate' Dominion Dennis XX 9591 on route 514 to Hayes *c*1924. The setting is the Uxbridge Road, with the tram tracks — always a hazard for cyclists — for LUT route 7 (Shepherd's Bush–Uxbridge) running down the centre of the road.

Above: Three Straker-Squires of the Edward Paul fleet, XO 8747 of 1923 leading.

Above right: This very curious picture is an official AEC photograph, and one can only assume it was taken either to warn of the hazards of B-type buses' trying to squeeze between oncoming trams, or, alternatively, to emphasise the manœuvrability of a bus compared to a tram. Despite its stated destination of Crouch End the bus is very much off-route, unlike the LUT 'W'-type trams, the setting indeed appearing to be Hampton Court.

Right: Pedestrians, seemingly heedless of the Golders Green B-type bus on route 2A attempting to make its way through them, head towards a row of four 'E1'-type LCC trams in Vauxhall Bridge Road *c*1920. Despite the attire of the smartly dressed gent on the far right, with his trilby, overcoat and newspaper, and several other women and men in full-length overcoats it must be a very warm day, judging by the uniformly fully wound-down upper-deck windows of all four cars.

track had suffered greatly during the war, and many of the trams were the best part of 20 years old. Although not yet worn out they would seem increasingly old-fashioned, their motor-bus contemporaries being long gone, replaced by something very much more advanced.

Although much the largest the LCC was far from being the only tram operator. Relations with the two biggest companies, the LUT and the MET — both part of the Underground group, to which the LGOC also belonged — were not particularly cordial, but the threat from the buses would draw them closer together. Then, to the east and south, there were the municipals — a mixed bunch that operated a motley assortment of cars, many of them primitive four-wheelers. Most worked joint services with the LCC, and by the early 1920s several were in dire financial straits. By the end of the decade the first cutbacks in the network would have taken place, and plans would be in hand for the replacement of the Kingston-area trams by trolleybuses.

On the Underground various improvements were in hand, including taking over lines from the main-line companies and electrifying them. Representing a major advance in technology was the introduction in 1920 of the first Tube trains with air-operated doors. Ordered in 1919 from Cammell Laird of Birkenhead, the 40 cars were destined for the Piccadilly Line, where the existing 1906 vintage motor cars, built with lattice gates, were rebuilt to conform with the newcomers. The old system had been highly labour-intensive, a gateman being needed to look after each pair of gates; now on a six-car train only two guards were required, in the trailing ends of each of the two motor cars. It might be argued that from an employment point of view this was a bad thing, as the 'land fit for heroes' was never able to guarantee all of them a job, but technological advances have always created this dilemma.

Although the ownership of a private car was becoming a possibility for the middle classes, the vast majority of the population was, throughout the decade, wholly reliant on public transport. At weekends huge crowds queued for buses, trams and trains to take them out to the country and bring them back again or for a trip to or on the river. Commercial flying was very much in its infancy, yet other popular bus or Underground-train destinations were Hendon, for flying displays, and Croydon, to watch the early biplane airliners taking off or landing, while it was still possible to board a passenger ship in the Pool of London for destinations within the British Isles such as Liverpool, Glasgow, Great Yarmouth and Newcastle.

Throughout the 1920s and the '30s the names of three men recur constantly in the developing saga of what was steadily becoming the most advanced public-transport system to be found anywhere. First there was Albert Stanley, created Baron Ashfield in 1914, and since 1910 Managing Director of the Underground Group. Next was Frank Pick, who in 1920 was Commercial Manager of the Group, in 1921 was appointed Assistant Managing Director and finally, in 1928, Managing Director, Ashfield remaining Chairman. The third was Charles Holden, the architect who provided London's transport system with some outstanding, iconic buildings, ranging from the spectacular headquarters of the Underground Group at 55 Broadway to suburban Underground stations. Anyone who ignores these remarkable characters and focuses solely on the technological advances of the era has missed the vital ingredient in the story.

Venn Street, Clapham, Easter 1920. Crowds queue patiently to board B type LF 8741 on route 107 for a day out in the Surrey countryside at Box Hill, near Dorking. Several of the adults, including at least one sailor-suited young gentleman, are holding children. One hopes there is room for all of them on the 34-seat bus, which is already filling up. Fortunately the day appears to be a fine one.

Above: Tilling-Stevens petrol-electric XH 9281 sets off from Caterham — then very much a Surrey country town — on the long journey to Camden Town on a sunny day in the summer of 1926.

Below: A photograph, taken from London Bridge *c*1925, of the Pool of London, then the busiest dock system in the world. In the foreground a paddle steamer of the General Steam Navigation Co has just left its berth and is setting off, its decks crowded with trippers, for Southend, whilst all around are lighters and tall-funnelled cargo ships. The long-established pleasure steamers could compete with the railway, the charabancs and motor coaches but not, post 1950, with the family motor car, and regular services would cease in the 1960s.

Left:
Lord Ashfield looks on indulgently at an award ceremony at an LGOC sports day in the mid-1920s. *London Transport*

Lower left:
A baby show at the LGOC Sports Gala, Stamford Bridge, 28 July 1923. Lord Ashfield is standing with an 'unidentified busman' who is holding his baby and accompanied by his wife who is clearly not going to let pass this opportunity to put on her glad rags. Lord Ashfield was in his element on such occasions.

Above:
Charles Holden.

Left:
Frank Pick.

15

Above: Lawrences' Garage in Brixton. Facilities such as this, providing everything the motorist could need, 'Day and Night', had by the end of the decade made pleasure motoring for the middle classes far more practical than hitherto and heralded an end to the monopoly that the train, the bus and the charabanc had between them enjoyed on trips from London to the country and seaside.

Above right: South Harrow station, 20 August 1926. Children on an outing from Shepherd's Bush have arrived on a train of District Line stock and are being marshalled for a day in the country, plenty of which still existed (although not for much longer) in the vicinity. There are a host of adults on hand, although just what function the uniformed chap with the drum — is he an Underground employee? — is needed to perform is a matter for speculation.

Right: Mechanics, a conductor (wearing his summertime white coat) and what look like office staff pose with a Daimler and, in the background, B2243, a single-decker on loan from the LGOC, inside a National garage in North East London c1923.

Above: Finsbury Park, 1922. A mother and son have just descended from open-top MET bogie 'A'-type tram No 73 of 1904 on route 31 to Tottenham Court Road, whilst covered-top 'H' type No 307 of 1909-12 is on its way north on route 29 to Enfield Town. Meanwhile a B-type bus belonging to Metropolitan and displaying a long-familiar advertisement swings in off a side road ahead of a horse and cart. It was here that London-bound trams changed from picking up their current from overhead to the conduit.

Left: Bargain-hunters in High Street, Kensington, waiting for the shops to open their doors and for the winter sales to begin, January 1922. In the distance a passenger is descending from what must have been a pretty chilly ride on the upper deck of a B type.

· 2 ·

The Tube — Replacing the Originals

LONDON had been the setting for the first tube railway in the world, when the City & South London was opened in November 1890 between Stockwell and King William Street, in the City of London. Its success encouraged others, although, as almost always with pioneers, they improved on its technology, and it was still trying to catch up in the 1920s. Its original locomotives and short (27ft), almost windowless, 'padded cell' carriages were archaic in the extreme, and, like the Central London Railway, opened in 1900 between

Shepherd's Bush and Bank, its tunnels were of a restricted diameter compared with the Hampstead, Piccadilly and Bakerloo tube lines of 1906/7.

Enter Charles Tyson Yerkes, the epitome of the 'up and at 'em' American entrepreneur; known as 'The Robber Baron', he was, according to Theodore Dreiser, 'not averse to bribery and blackmail' and was the driving force behind the construction and operation of London's tube railways. He it was who set up the Underground Electric Railways Company of London Ltd (commonly known as the London Electric Railway), which by 1920, when our story opens, had absorbed very underground or tube concern save the Metropolitan Railway. Born in Philadelphia in 1837, Yerkes had been imprisoned after his distinctly shaky financial empire had collapsed as a result of the Chicago Fire of 1871. Nothing daunted, he used his connections, extending right up to the White House, to get out of jail and set about making a fresh start. This included trading in his wife of 22 years for a 24-year-old and gaining control of most of the Chicago transport system. Thwarted in his attempt to get the lot, in 1900 he turned his attentions to London. No doubt he felt it would do him no harm to emulate the British aristocracy and the man who was about to become King Edward VII, and although accompanied by wife number two he quickly acquired an official mistress and several others kept in reserve. One of the reasons why few of those who travelled regularly on his trains and trams followed his example was the cost, although one cannot for a moment imagine that Mr Pooter would have so mistreated his beloved Carrie.

Despite all his extra-curricular activities Yerkes managed to set up in a very short time practically all the tube lines which still serve Londoners, before

Frank Pick (left) and Lord Ashfield, pictured c1923.

dying in the Waldorf Astoria Hotel in New York in 1905 — just in time, some suggested, to escape the wrath of his American shareholders consequent upon their profits' reaching nothing like the heights he had predicted. The British investors were more cautious, having a much closer acquaintance with the reality of the situation; the Underground railways never were anything like as profitable as the buses.

The day was saved by none other than Lord Ashfield. — except that in 1907 this title was seven years away, he at the time being merely 32-year-old Albert Stanley of Derbyshire and Detroit. Not that 'merely' in any way does justice to this remarkable man. Appointed General Manager, with the handsome salary of £2,000 per annum, he teamed up with George Gibb, Managing Director, and Frank Pick, a young lawyer who became Publicity Officer, with responsibility for marketing, both having been headhunted from the North Eastern Railway. By 1908 the UERL was making a working profit. Stanley succeeded Gibb as Managing Director in 1910, being knighted for his services to London's transport in 1914, and by 1920 Lord Ashfield and Pick, who had revealed an astonishingly broad vision on all aspects of design as well as a superb grasp of detail, had formed themselves into a team which over the next 20 years was to prove unmatched in the field of public transport.

Ashfield understood perfectly what being head of a vast public-transport undertaking entailed. Anthony Bull CBE, who rose to become Vice-Chairman of London Transport, applied for a job with the Underground Group in 1924 and was taken to meet Lord Ashfield, 'to discuss what I should read at Cambridge University. Lord Ashfield explained that it was not of great importance … because the basic job … was epitomised by two men selling their labour — one at the front of the bus, who was called the driver, and one at the rear, who was called a conductor. It was managing that labour which was important to the London Underground Group … since 1912 it was the buses, which were earning a profit, that were supporting the underground railways, which were operating at a loss. '

Trevor Hearing, who worked with Pick in the 1930s, recalled a talk which Pick gave to the Chief Officers of London Transport and which beautifully encapsulates his philosophy — 'Do not be afraid of a spice of vice, a spark of irrationality, a fondness for inconsistency, a flash of genius.' In 1916 Pick asked Edward Johnston to develop a typeface for the Underground and in 1918 to redesign the roundel symbol. This redesigned symbol and variations of the Johnston Sans typeface became classics, still in use in London today and copied all over the world. In Pick's own words, 'The test of the goodness of

A poster by Jeffryes for the Underground, 1929. No biographical details — not even a surname — appear to have survived of this artist, the style an example of the best graphic design of the period, much encouraged by Frank Pick. *London Transport Museum*

a thing is its fitness for use. If it fails on this first test, no amount of ornamentation or finish will make it any better; it will only make it more expensive, more foolish.' Pick encouraged fine design in every aspect of the undertaking, and the posters from the 1920s and '30s have become classics, reproduced again and again. Pick understood the value of good publicity. It didn't come cheap — in 1924 Pick spent no less than £70,795 on the press bureau, traffic advertising and other publicity items — but the artists he employed created classics and set standards for the rest to follow.

One of the results of Yerkes' influence was that the great majority of trains operating the tube and underground lines in 1920 had a distinctly trans-atlantic appearance. Similar-looking, although decked out in different colour schemes, the all-steel cars of the Hampstead, Bakerloo and Piccadilly lines were built in the USA, Hungary and France, although some were assembled in England. Likewise the District Line trains, although built by Brush at Loughborough, would not have looked out of place on the elevated lines of New York or Chicago. Their curved top windows, flat, wooden-planked sides, clerestory roofs and rattan seats all emphasised their American design, and they were almost identical to some placed in service in New York.

In 1920 the Metropolitan Railway, which considered itself (with some justification) virtually a main-line company, was operating a considerable variety of stock, none of it much influenced by America. It ranged from both clerestory-and elliptical-roof sets of cars, with the usual open layout and end doors, some of which originally had open ends but which were soon enclosed, to sets of arc-roof, compartment carriages. Some of these were powered by motor cars, others hauled both by steam or electric locomotives. There was also modern, elliptical-roof compartment stock, as well as a set of the original, rigid, eight-wheel carriages of 1866, retained for use on the remote, rural Brill branch, and, at the other extreme, two Pullmans, which ran between Verney Junction, Aylesbury, Chesham and Baker Street and

the City, these last having been introduced in an effort to lure affluent First-class 'Metroland' passengers from the Great Central Railway.

The first new trains of the decade were 40 cars for the Piccadilly Line, fitted with air-operated automatic doors and placed in service in 1920. There had been some earlier cars with fully enclosed doors, including a set in the centre as well as at each end, but the original Yerkes stock, with its labour-intensive end gates and no central access, still formed the great majority of tube stock. The 1920 cars were a big step forward; from then on all new stock featured automatic doors, and the older stock was gradually converted. However, the lack of grab-poles, the thick centre-door pillars, concrete floors, sombre leather upholstery covering some pretty uncomfortable seats, the absence of arm rests and the racket made by the trains as they rattled through the tunnels were all features which Frank Pick, who took a particular interest in train design, found unacceptable and was determined to do something about. The result was the Standard Tube Stock, ordered in 1923 after evaluation of prototype vehicles, and which would eventually number 1,466 cars.

The new era first made itself apparent in 1921 at Golders Green depot, where a wooden mock-up of a driving control car, built by the engineering staff there, and a number of accompanying engineering drawings were unveiled. This was followed by the ordering, in August 1922, of six prototype cars from five different manufacturers. Tube-train contracts were much sought after, not least for the large numbers involved, and all the cars were delivered early in 1923. All were essentially very similar, although the Gloucester Railway Carriage & Wagon Co's No 820 incorporated the greatest variations. Shown to the press in February 1923, they looked ultra-modern in their handsome livery of bright red and white with black lining and maroon doors and were much admired, even being referred to as 'Underground Pullman specials', which was slightly over the top. Orders were placed almost immediately for an initial 191 cars. By the time I got to travel on them in the 1940s they seemed very old-fashioned, both inside and out, compared to their successors, the 1938 stock, and about as far removed from the Pullman concept as could be imagined — a point which serves to illustrates not merely the lack of historical awareness of an eight-year-old but also how rapidly tube-train design progressed in the 1920s and '30s.

Internally the new stock was a huge improvement, and this is where Pick's hand showed most clearly. Wooden slats replaced concrete floors, there was traverse as well as longitudinal seating, upholstered in the Underground Group's standard 'lozenge' pattern and fitted with arm rests, and there were grab rails and draught screens. Bodies were of steel, with aluminium doors. The cab was of a much neater design than anything yet seen on a tube train, with manually operated doors on either side and in the centre of the front, with unequal-size windows, being virtually flush with the metal panelling on either side; the asymmetrical front was so designed to accommodate a two-line indicator box with destination plates behind the glass. The unique conditions resulting from trains' spending much of their journeys in tunnels ensured that the clerestory roof would remain a feature long after it had ceased to be built into main-line stock and would not finally disappear from the Underground system until 1971 (and even later on the Isle of Wight, whither some Standard Stock trains migrated in 1967). The one retrograde feature of a tube train that advancing technology could not yet eliminate was the location of the electrical equipment, which still had to be situated above floor level, the two ranks of ventilator slats between the cab and the passenger compartment of every motor car a prominent reminder of the fact that the equipment occupied one quarter of the entire car.

Production of Standard Stock continued throughout the 1920s and into the 1930s, the last emerging in 1934. Meanwhile improvements were carried out on the Yerkes-era stock which was to be kept in service. Gates disappeared, replaced by automatic sliding doors, and Pick-style interiors were installed. In 1922 the Euston–Moorgate section of the City & South London Railway was closed so that the tunnels could be enlarged. It reopened in April 1924, following which trains began to run via Camden Town to Highgate and Hendon; three months later an extension was opened from Hendon Central to Edgware. The stations were designed by the company's architect, Stanley A. Heaps. Built of brick with pitched, tiled roofs, they were described as being of 'a suburban style in keeping with housing developments'. Some still survive, although Colindale was destroyed during World War 2, whilst others have been altered and incorporated into later extensions. They were pleasant buildings, if less striking than those of Holden, with whom Heaps would work during the London Transport era in designing depots and other buildings.

At the end of November 1923 the southern section of the City & South London from Moorgate to Clapham Common was closed for enlargement to standard tube size. It reopened in December 1924. Two years later there followed the extension to what is still the most southerly outpost of the Underground network, with the opening of the Clapham Common–Morden section, all of it in tunnel. Trains now ran all the way from Edgware to Morden, the section in tunnel from East Finchley via Bank to Morden, at 17¼ miles, being the longest continuous train journey that could be made anywhere in the world without seeing daylight.

Morden was typical of many Home Counties rural communities which would by the end of the 1920s find themselves becoming part of suburbia. A Surrey village of some 1,000 souls, it was situated beside the 125-acre grounds of Morden Hall, where until 1922 a pair of 18th-century water mills had been occupied in grinding snuff. Today the grounds belong to the National Trust, given it in 1941 by the last owner, Gilliat Edward Hatfield, described by the Trust as 'a generous and kind man with a great love for people'. The mill buildings and even the water wheel are still there, and the park, with its expanse of meadows through which flows the River Wandle, once fished by Isaac Walton, and avenues of magnificent trees, some five minutes' walk from the tube station and bounded to the north by Tramlink, is a glorious rural oasis deep in suburbia. The River Wandle might be said to have been the cradle of industry prior to the Industrial Revolution, for in the late 18th century there were around 50 mills, powered by some 90 water wheels, in its 13-mile length. Deeply polluted when my father was a keeper in Wandle Park in the 1960s, it has seen a remarkable renaissance of late, with an abundance of fish, including trout, returning.

Right: Morden residents, 1924.

Below: The wheel of the water mill at Morden Hall, which until 1924 was used to power the snuff mills.

In some respects Morden is typical of what happened in the London suburbs between the wars, when, as housing developments spread apace, encouraged by extensions to the Underground and improving bus services, there remained sizeable green areas — sometimes donated by generous patrons, sometimes provided by local authorities (and particularly the London County Council, which bought up large tracts well beyond its own area, notably Epping Forest and Coulsdon Common) and sometimes by accident, so that, viewed from above from an airliner landing at Croydon, Heston or Hendon — or today a satellite image — the amount of green is astonishing. For all that, the spread of suburbia throughout the 1920s was something to behold, and naming avenues of 'Tudorbethan' semi-detacheds after beauty spots in the Lake District did not lessen their impact on what had once been countryside.

Charles Holden, 'one of the first of the moderns' according to John Betjeman, received his initial commission from Frank Pick in 1924 to redesign the façade of Bond Street station; Morden was his first completely new structure for the Underground Group, and the Portland-stone station, standing boldly at the centre of its accompanying parade of

Above: Morden, 8 July 1927. A small girl poses for the photographer at the corner of a newly completed row of houses, at least two of which boast some 'Tudorbethan' woodwork embellishments. The houses on the opposite side of the road — possibly one named after a beauty spot in the Lake District (hence, no doubt, the grass which has been allowed to flourish at the pavements' edge) — have yet to be completed.

Below: Morden station shortly after completion in June 1927. Parked in the remarkably sparsely populated forecourt beyond the hand-operated petrol pump are an open-top S-type double-decker, with solid tyres, and a K-type single-decker with pneumatic tyres.

Interior of Morden station.

shops, represents a landmark of 20th-century architecture. Less celebrated than Holden's later stations in North and West London (perhaps because after the war a large office block was built above the station and parade of shops, reducing its impact somewhat), it retains its distinctive circular entrance hall, with its elegant light fittings and bold Underground roundel filling the window.

Holden and Pick were wholly in accord. Holden believed that architecture should 'throw off its mantle of deceits; its cornices, pilasters, mouldings'; that it should be 'functional and accessible'. Serving with Lutyens on the War Graves Commission, Holden designed a vast range of buildings, from Bristol Central Library (which is said to have had an influence on Rennie Mackintosh's Glasgow Art School) to the Senate House of London University — 'London's first skyscraper' — and the head-quarters of the Underground Group at 55 Broadway, to which we shall return. Twice refusing a knight-hood, because he believed that architecture should be a collaborative effort, he was a man who inspired admiration and great affection.

Within five years of the arrival of the Under-ground the population of Morden had increased to exceed 12,000, and the forecourt had become the terminus for a number of bus routes. In its early days the bold, clean lines of the station served to heighten the antique appearance of the open-top, open-staircase, solid-tyred NS double-deckers parked outside: nor during the 1940s and early '50s did the wartime austerity-specification D-class Daimlers, all 181 of which were at one time or another housed at nearby Merton garage, gain from the comparison, and it was only in the mid-1950s, when the RT family achieved supremacy, that a bus was found with lines to match the elegant simplicity of Holden's masterpiece.

Above: The strikingly modern and uncluttered exterior of East Finchley station, designed by Charles Holden and C. H. Bucknell.

Left: The forecourt of Morden station on Derby Day (11 May) 1929. The two inspectors are standing in the bays where passengers who have alighted from the tube trains wait to board their buses for the race meeting. In the background, to the west of the station, four K types stand beside the parade of shops then in the course of construction. *London Transport*

Above: Golders Green station in the early 1920s. B and K types await passengers, whilst beyond is an MET 'A'-type tram built by Brush and dating from 1904. *London Transport*

Above right: Sudbury Town station, Piccadilly Line. The date is 24 April 1926, Cup Final day, and four NS buses are parked on the forecourt ready to convey people to Wembley stadium. *London Transport*

Right: The original caption purports this to be an everyday scene of passengers alighting from and boarding 'Gate' stock at the Elephant & Castle Northern and Bakerloo Line station in 1924. If this is so then they must have been the slowest-moving group of customers ever encountered on the Underground system. *London Transport*

Above: Charing Cross station, District Line, 13 October 1921. Then, as now, the Underground was never backward in coming forward with a mixture of informative and advertising information. The directions for the Tube and the South Eastern & Chatham Railway platforms are clear and simple, as are the typefaces used on the football posters. Most London professional teams were close to Underground stations; of those featured here Crystal Palace is the exception, although it will at last be on the network when the extension of the East London line from New Cross Gate to Norwood Junction and West Croydon is completed.
London Transport

Above: Edgware depot in 1925, with three 1923-stock trains flanking two of original 1907 vintage.
London Transport

Below: A 1926 Standard-stock Piccadilly Line train at Hammersmith.

· 3 ·

The Surface Lines

I N 1920 steam still had a presence on the Underground, although strictly speaking it was only north of Harrow that passengers could still travel in a steam-hauled Underground train. Elsewhere, for example, GNR and Midland Railway steam-hauled passenger trains worked through the tunnels of the Widened Lines to Moorgate, the GWR worked through the Inner Circle tunnels to Smithfield meat market, and the occasional special ventured through Brunel's Thames Tunnel on its way to the seaside via New Cross or New Cross Gate, while engineers' trains on the Metropolitan and District lines would feature steam for decades to come.

A new era began in 1920 on the District Line with the introduction of the 'F' stock. Far removed from Yerkes' American-style stock, these wide, all-steel cars looked just as modern as the Standard-stock tube vehicles. Each smooth side, curving into an elliptical roof, had three sets of sliding doors, hand-operated at first but converted in the 1930s to air operation. A very small, oval window sufficed for the motorman to look through. Internally they were not particularly comfortable or attractive — something that irked Frank Pick, who had them refurbished and much improved, and the last would not be withdrawn until 1963.

Left: A December 1922 picture of a seven-car train of 1915-vintage gate-end stock of the Central London Railway, approaching Ealing Broadway. The 4¼-mile extension from Wood Lane to Ealing Broadway was opened on 3 August 1920. This had is origins in a Great Western Railway freight-only line, opened in 1917, a spur being built to Wood Lane, and was just about the nearest the GWR ever came to operating electric trains. *London Transport*

Above: One of the Bakerloo Line Watford-stock motor cars, designed jointly by the London Electric Railway and the London & North Western Railway, ordered in 1914 but not delivered until 1920, and painted in LNWR livery. These cars did away with the gates and instead had inward-swinging doors which were designed to spring back closed. By 1917 the Bakerloo Line was running between the Elephant & Castle and Watford Junction, the northern section being over LNWR track. The LNWR did not start its Euston–Watford electric service until 1922, a year before the company ceased to exist, although the trains it employed, in some respects enlarged versions of the Tube trains, would last well into British Railways days, one of the motor cars surviving to be preserved as part of the National Collection. *London Transport*

The next group of cars were the 'Gs' of 1923, which, although they would ultimately outlast the 'Fs', looked far more old-fashioned. The clerestory returned, and the sides were totally flat, but Pick ensured that the interiors, similar to those of contemporary tube cars, were a real advance — which was, of course, the passenger's first priority. Even better were the 101 'K'-class cars of 1928-30. Although they, too, featured a clerestory roof, this sloped down to the front to give a much neater appearance, and the entire aspect, inside and out, was

smoother and more modern. Pick, who by the time the last 'K' appeared was Managing Director, had done an excellent job.

The Metropolitan Railway continued to pursue its independent way throughout the 1920s. During the 1914-18 war patronage had increased dramatically on the Inner Circle, worked jointly with the District Railway, and in 1921 39 trailer and 20 motor cars were introduced, mostly for the Inner Circle service, on which trains were increased from four to five cars. They worked alongside earlier stock, including the

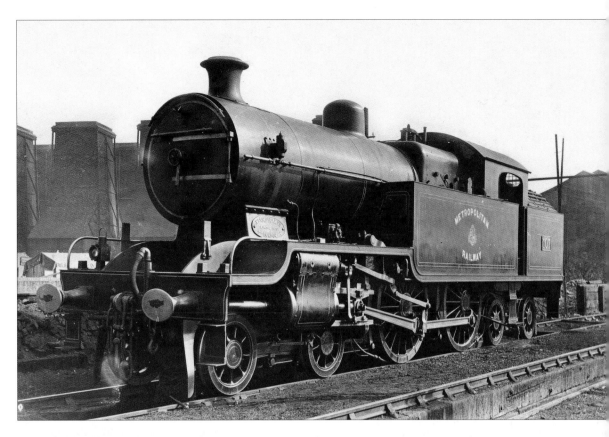

Left: A poster for Winter Sales, designed for the Underground by H. S. Williamson in 1924. Harold Sandys Williamson was a key figure in the art world of the time. Born in 1892, he attended Leeds and the Royal Academy schools before serving in World War 1, being wounded several times and becoming an official war artist. Later appointed Principal of Chelsea Art School, he offered part-time teaching posts to a number of up-and-coming young artists, including Henry Moore, Ceri Richards and William Roberts — a tradition that was still being maintained when the author was a student there in the 1960s. *London Transport Museum*

Above: No 107, one of the handsome 'H'-class 4-4-4Ts. Eight of these locomotives were built by Kerr, Stuart & Co in 1921 for the Metropolitan Railway, hauling passenger trains beyond Rickmansworth. *Ian Allan Library*

original clerestory roof cars of 1904, and could also be seen, for example, on the East London and Hammersmith lines. By now the Metropolitan had given up the clerestory for good, but a feature from the early days with which it persisted (and which nowadays seems extraordinary) was First-class travel. Rather less surprisingly it also retained this on the compartment-type carriages, 42 of which entered service in 1921 for the 'long-distance' services out into the Chiltern stockbroker belt and countryside. Electrification was extended from Harrow to Rickmansworth in January 1925, while

November of that year saw the opening of the Watford branch, with an intermediate station at Croxley Green; for a time services on the latter were shared with the LNER, which ran steam trains to Marylebone, but these ceased at the end of 1926, when the service became all-electric. The following year 12 new compartment-type, Third-class motor coaches entered service. These were designed to work with existing trailer cars, and various rearrangements of units and rebuildings followed, whilst in 1929 a further 30 motor cars and 25 trailers were ordered.

Locomotives were not unknown in the very early days of Underground electrification, but only on the Metropolitan Railway did they establish a significant and long-term presence. By the end of World War 1 the Metropolitan's original 20 centre-cab double-bogie locomotives were proving somewhat under-powered, and in 1919 two were rebuilt. However, the frames proved unable to cope with the additional weight, and so new build was decided upon. Thus was commissioned, from Vickers of Barrow, what was to become a very celebrated design, two examples of which are still with us. Bo-Bos of 1,200hp, with a top speed of 65mph, they proved exactly what was needed for the long runs out to Rickmansworth. Handsome in appearance, with stylishly pointed cab fronts rather reminiscent of the LSWR electric units, and painted in traditional Met chocolate with black and yellow lining, all 20 were given names, recalling a diverse cast of London characters from the past, among them Florence Nightingale, Dick Whittington and Benjamin Disraeli. All, that is, save No 15 *Wembley*, a name it acquired when exhibited at the Wembley Empire Exhibition in 1924.

Above: One of the two Pullman cars, built by the Birmingham Railway Carriage & Wagon Co for the Metropolitan Railway in 1909, after repainting in 1922/3 from the original and difficult-to-maintain original chocolate and cream livery to all-over crimson lake. On the far right of the group is the Metropolitan Railway's General Manager, J. S. Anderson, whilst the elderly gent with the stick is Lord Aberconway, its Chairman. *London Transport*

Above right: A Gloucester-built 'G'-class motor car of 1923. *Ian Allan Library*

Right: Interior of a 'G'-class District Line car, built by the Gloucester Railway Carriage & Wagon Co in 1923. *London Transport*

Above: L34, one of the venerable Beyer, Peacock 4-4-0Ts of 1880/1, as modified with a cab and still at work for the District Railway at the end of the 1920s. *H. C. Casserley*

Below: No 81, one of the seven 'E'-class 0-4-4Ts built for the Metropolitan Railway between 1986 and 1901. No 1 of this class has been preserved and can be seen at work at that remote outpost of the Met, Quainton Road. *Ian Allan Library*

Above: A Chesham-bound train of the Metropolitan Railway at Wembley Park in the early 1920s. The train consists of five 'Dreadnought' carriages plus one of the two Pullmans and is hauled by No 14, one of the Vickers-built locomotives of 1922, which as yet has no nameplates fitted. *Ian Allan Library*

Below: A Metropolitan Railway seven-car train on 1921 stock, photographed near Rickmansworth in 1925. The leading vehicle is No 198, the prototype for the later 'MW' stock. *London Transport*

This purports to show an 'automatic' booking machine at Leicester Square station on 14 April 1921. It was, however, not completely automatic, for the jolly chap, who was not actually inside the machine, had to 'push one of a series of buttons for the correct fare', whereupon 'the ticket would be dispensed straight into the passenger's hand'.

'Bright Young Things' by Maurice Greiffenhagen,
a poster commissioned by the railway companies in 1924.

Interior of Metropolitan Line train of 1923 stock. *London Transport*

Underground poster by Dudley Jarrett
for the 1926 Royal Tournament.
London Transport Museum

• 4 •

Whither the Tram?

LCC pocket map and timetable for 1927.

BY 1920 London's huge tram network was virtually complete. But it was not in a particularly healthy state. Right from the start it had faced two enormous disadvantages. Firstly neither the City of London nor the City of Westminster would allow the disruption to its streets of the laying of tram tracks, nor did it want the somewhat downmarket image a tram line evoked of being a conveyance of vast numbers of working- or lower-class people. Secondly, where tracks were allowed on the very fringes of the City and Westminster and in the inner suburbs the authorities insisted that there should be no unsightly poles and overhead wires, and therefore the very expensive conduit system had to be employed.

In the earliest days of the electric tram it was so far ahead of the opposition — which consisted of either horse buses or the very early, unreliable, uncomfortable, small-capacity, petrol-powered motor buses — that these disadvantages did not matter. But the tide had begun to turn in 1910 with the introduction of the B-type motor bus, and the latter's reliability and flexibility — and its appearance on every main thoroughfare in the City and West End — was causing the tramways severe headaches. In 1921 the LCC had to rescue the Borough of Leyton system from virtual collapse, and in 1926 *Tramway and Railway World* noted that the Metropolitan Electric Tramways, perhaps the most *avant-garde* of the London concerns, was in such a parlous financial state that 'it has not been able to keep the track [which it operated on behalf of Middlesex County Council] in repair as stipulated and … for fifteen years no rent has been paid'.

In December 1920, at Electric Railway House on Broadway, Frank Pick read a paper, 'Competition in Urban Transport', which looked in detail at the relationship of the tram to the bus. It is full of fascinating statistics and observations; we will quote a few. 'In the year 1920 that is now closing it is estimated that the underground railways will have carried 675 millions of passengers, the suburban

Neither the first nor the last time a traffic jam had been observed at the Elephant & Castle. The date is sometime in 1920, and the bowler-hatted gentleman clearly has plenty of time to negotiate the crossroads as B1576 of Leyton garage, working the 35B (and rather slower off the mark than its unidentified companion a short way ahead), has to give way to a line of LCC tramcars led by two 'C'-class four-wheelers, No 205 being the second car. A line of bogie 'Es' and 'E1s' follow. The 'Cs' were built especially for the inauguration of the Elephant & Castle–Greenwich/New Cross/Deptford routes in 1904. By 1920 their riding had become distinctly lively, but this was partly cured later in the decade, when they were fitted with hydraulic suspension. All were withdrawn in the late 1920s and early '30s, being replaced on the hilly Dulwich routes to which some of them had migrated by the 'HR2s'. *London Transport*

steam and electric railways 350 millions, the tramways or street railways 1,100 millions and the motor omnibuses 1,035 millions.' By the second paragraph it is clear that the tramways are going to come out of this review badly. 'The horse omnibus occupied in the past those streets in London which are now traversed by electric tramways. The tramway is the usurper.' Pick then quotes his boss, Lord Ashfield, and invites him to deliver a telling blow. 'Once a city passes a certain size, the street-railway solution of the traffic problem is seen not to have been the right one. The street railway is an intermediate solution good until a more highly specialised scheme of transport facilities is wanted.' Meaning that the ultimate solution to moving really large numbers of people around a city was either a surface or an underground railway.

Pick had just visited the United States and was struck by how ill suited to public transport were London streets by comparison. 'One reason why London has remained a motor-omnibus city is the narrowness of its main streets, and the irregularity of its planning. One would have thought that an arterial road of a city carrying a tramway would have been of a width sufficient for the movement of three lines of

traffic in each direction, of which the two centre lines would have mainly consisted of street cars. London is a shameful way behind such a standard. London has tramways which ought never to have been constructed as they are.'

Some UK cities, notably Liverpool and, to a lesser extent, Leeds, did provide wide avenues, with the

Above: 'E1' No 1762, a representative of London's standard tram for the best part of 50 years, the first entering service in 1907, the last, of a class numbering precisely 1,000, in 1930. No 1762, with a body built by Hurst Nelson, came out in 1921. It is seen here in High Street, Croydon, on its way from Purley — then virtually in the country — to the Embankment. Through-running between the LCC and Croydon Corporation systems had begun on Sunday 7 February 1926, when the 6in gap at Norbury between the rails of the two systems was connected. The scene has changed remarkably little except that instead of heading along the High Street to North End trams now cross from George Street to Crown Hill, in front of the Tudor almshouses, the roofs and chimneys of which are just visible to the right of No 1762, whilst behind the ornate, listed façade of Grants department store (on the left of the picture) is now a modern entertainment complex.

Above right: The LUT's answer to the 'E1'. No 324 was one of 40 'T'-type bogie trams dating from 1906. These were known as 'palace' cars on account of the high standard of construction and interior appointments — despite their open balconies and lack of windscreens, the latter a Metropolitan Police requirement. No 324 is working the Uxbridge Road service, which would be taken over in the early 1930s by the 'Felthams' (and upon which, at the beginning of the 21st century, there would be serious proposals to reinstate trams). Note the wonderfully varied display of advertisements; that for Bovril sounds like a threat! Zena Dare, the star of the 1929 production of Cynara, was one of the most famous British musical theatre actresses of all time. Born in 1887, her career began in the West End in the Edwardian era; 50 years later she was still starring, playing the role of Eliza Dolittle in the original stage production of *My Fair Lady*, and was the only leading member of the cast to remain throughout its 5½-year run. When it finally closed in 1963 she retired from the stage at the age of 76; she died at the age of 88. The King's Theatre, Hammersmith, dating from 1902, was one of many built by W. G. R. Sprague, the leading theatre designer of his time. It was demolished in 1963, but a fine example of Sprague's work, the Aldwych, has survived. *London Transport*

Right: The rather pleasant interior of a 'T'-type car, managing to sport as many advertisements within as without, photographed at Hanwell depot on a sunny June day in 1925. *Ian Allan Library*

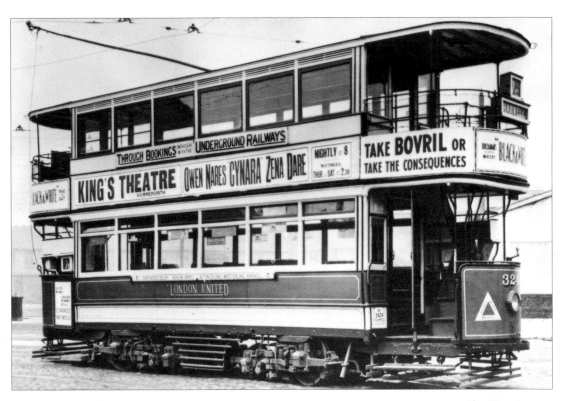

USED EVERYWHERE

tram tracks running along a central reservation, and these ensured their systems' survival into the 1950s. Such favourable conditions were absent in London. When, in the 1990s, trams returned to the streets of London in the form of the Croydon Tramlink the lessons had been learned, and they ran either on former railway land or along streets from which other traffic had largely been banished.

The difference in operating cost between tram and bus was negligible, but the tram suffered in that its capital cost was more than three times greater. Typical of Pick is the following statement, and remember that it was made in 1920. 'The danger to the motor-omnibus industry seems to centre in the fuel problem. The world stocks of oil seem less than the world stocks of coal. There is a time calculated to be not very far off when the oil will be exhausted. Fortunately the use of petrol substitutes throws open a wide future.'

The MET and the LUT were part of Ashfield's and Pick's Underground Group and were the most progressive of all the tramway operators, although the LCC was the largest and was deeply committed to the tram. The LCC General Manager, Joshua Bruce, did his best and in 1924 began a programme of improving its vast fleet. This was called 'Pullmanisation' — a term also applied to contemporary underground trains (and equally misleading). It consisted of upholstering all the seats (although upstairs wooden backs were retained) and brightening up the interiors and exteriors. The trouble with the London tram was that it was built to last, and the great

Above: A poster for Wotan and Tantalum lamps, featuring a well-lit Houses of Parliament, equally well-lit trams crossing Westminster Bridge, and a rather dimly lit paddle-steamer emerging from beneath it.
London Transport Museum

Above right: Lines of LCC 'E'- and 'E1'-class cars heading east and west along the Embankment *c*1929. No 492 (left), working route 26, is an 'E' of 1906, destined to be withdrawn by 1938, whilst No 1032, on route 36, is a slightly more modern 'E1' of 1907/8 which will last into the 1950s.

Right: A picture taken at the very beginning of the 1930s but featuring a highly varied collection of vehicles in the Mile End Road — all except the T-class Green Line coach and the LT bus (although the first examples of both types had appeared in 1929) dating from the 1920s or earlier. Prominent is East Ham Corporation tram No 52, basically a standard LCC 'E1', delivered from Brush in 1927. It is having its 'plough' inserted for the remainder of its journey on conduit power into the City of London, whilst a motor van and a horse-powered dray piled high with straw bales inch past over the stone setts. Clearly neither horse nor tram are aiding the flow of traffic, but their demise in the decades to come would do little to alleviate the situation.
London Transport

Right: A fine model of one of the original West Ham Milnes four-wheelers new in 1903/4 and later fitted with a covered top.
The exhortation to support municipal transport was applied frequently by authorities throughout the country.

Right: South Metropolitan car No 29 could hardly claim to be a shining example of modern urban transport by the late 1920s, when this picture was taken. Built for Croydon Corporation by Brush in 1902, it was transferred four years later to the South Met and is seen here working the Tooting–Croydon service. With unupholstered seats on both decks, upper deck and staircases exposed to the elements, battered paneling and faded paintwork (and with no attempt at modernisation since it first saw the light of day, one year after the death of Queen Victoria), it only just staggered into the 1930s and would be sold for scrap by London Transport after spending several years in store.

Above: Reeves Corner, Croydon, *c*1929. Nearest the camera and heading towards Sutton is South Metropolitan No 9, a Brush-built four-wheeler of 1906, which will carry straight on rather than swinging to the right like the ex-LUT 'U'-type bogie car (dating from 1902) on its way to Tooting.

Below: Metropolitan No 141, one of the 20 four-wheel, 36-seat 'E'-type single-deck cars built by Brush in 1905 for the lightly trafficked Alexandra Palace routes, at Wood Green depot in July 1924.

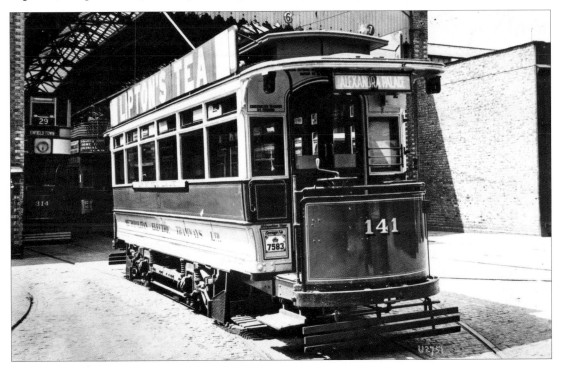

SHOP EARLY

RIDE IN COMFORT BY LONDON'S TRAMWAYS

A 1928 poster by Rowles, featuring the rather comfortable — and possibly 'Pullmanised' — nicely upholstered lower deck of a bogie tram. The model tank engine has a somewhat unusual wheel arrangement. *London Transport Museum*

majority of these 'E'- and 'E1'-type cars dated back to Edwardian times. Some 124 'E1s' were added to the fleet in 1922, and even then the class was not complete, for a further 50, using equipment from withdrawn 'F'- and 'G'-class single-deckers, were introduced in 1930. These single-deckers worked the Kingsway Subway routes, but at the end of the decade the subway was closed so that it could be enlarged to take double-deck cars. Yet even the new 'E3s', which worked the subway and other routes, and the 'HR2s', for hilly routes (and based on the 'HR1s' of 1929), although powerful and in other ways slightly updated, internally represented no great advance over the Edwardian concept of a tramcar.

Meanwhile the Underground Group was taking a far deeper look at the form a modern tram should take. Christopher Spencer, the group's Tramway Manager, had been one of Pick's party which had visited the USA in 1919, and came back much impressed with what he had seen. Like Pick he expressed his thoughts in a paper, published in 1925. Referring to the increasing public criticism of trams, he commented: 'This is not surprising, because there has been generally no noticeable alteration made as regards external appearance, and although the equipment has been vastly improved the only visible difference internally has been the use of white paint.' He went on to explain how it might 'evolve out of the chrysalis state of being chiefly the workman's vehicle', and the first results were two experimental trams introduced in 1926. The LGOC built the body of one at Chiswick, the MET the other at Hendon. There is not space here to go into the details of these cars other than to note that they led to the finest fleet of trams found anywhere in the UK at the time, the 'Felthams', so called because they were built by the Union Construction & Finance Co, part of the Underground Group, at its Feltham works.

Designed by W. S. Graf-Baker, Assistant Engineer of the Underground Group's railways, the first two prototypes, Nos 320 and 330, appeared in April and October 1929 respectively. (There must have been something in the air or water, for in the same year the LGOC introduced its almost-as-revolutionary AEC Regent, Renown and Regal buses.) Nos 320 and 330, with their all-steel-and-aluminium construction, sleek lines, fully enclosed cabs (with a seat for the driver), maximum-traction bogies and an interior designed to allow free flow of passengers, instantly made every other tram — and, indeed, bus — look old-fashioned. The third prototype, No 331 is just outside our time frame, making its debut in June 1930, but we may note that most fortunately it has survived and can be sampled at the National Tramway Museum at Crich, Derbyshire. Two of the production batch of 100 also survive, one in the USA, the other in the London Transport collection.

Above: The Thornton Heath Pond headquarters of Croydon Corporation Tramways, with the depot at the side, *c*1929. The wooden cabin marked 'CCT' was where the inspector controlling the points for the local 42 route, curving away from the main 16/18 route, took up residence. A wreath has been placed over the war memorial, so the photograph was probably taken in November. *London Transport*

Left: Ernest George Coppes Gilbert of East Finchley learning how to drive a tram at the controls of MET service car No 2 in Hendon depot sometime in the 1920s. *London Transport*

Above: The MET's impressive-looking 'Bluebell', No 318 of 1927. So named because of its livery of light blue and cream, it was better than anything the LCC could offer, being fully enclosed — although there was still no glazing for the driver's windscreen — and featuring platform doors and an unusually low step height. Extensive use of aluminium sheeting meant a noticeable reduction in weight over previous large bogie cars, as well as enhanced performance. Passengers boarded at the front and alighted at the rear. Fitted with air brakes, it was unfortunately involved in a serious accident on Barnet Hill on 17 June 1927, when it failed to stop and hit the back of a lorry, resulting in the death of the motorman, Maurice Kent. Following considerable modification it returned to service but because of its unique character did not long survive the LPTB takeover, being scrapped in 1936. It did, however, lead to the magnificent 'Felthams'. *London Transport*

Above right: The dawn of a new era. Cliché this may be, but it must surely describe precisely the reaction of this crowd of eager passengers as they board prototype 'Feltham' No 320 of 1929 at Golders Green. Is it too much to claim that if a 'Feltham' suddenly appeared from the Shirley direction and pulled up at the Tramlink stop at East Croydon in 2009, whilst note would certainly be taken of its being a double-decker, few would recoil and comment about its lack of modernity? Presumably the lady with the fox fur has not just retrieved it from a nasty end under a tube train. Fur was obviously in fashion in Golders Green in June 1929, for the MET official, taking care where he places his hand, is ushering a lady with a rather more modest fur collar towards No 320. *London Transport*

Right: Lower-deck interior of prototype centre-entrance 'Feltham'.

<h1 align="center">• 5 •</h1>

<h1 align="center">Bus Scene 1920</h1>

FROM the earliest days of the motor bus certain types have become synonymous with London. The Routemaster, a 1950s design, did not cease normal service until 2005, while its predecessor, the RT, served London for 40 years,

Flanders and Swann sang of the 'Big Six-wheeler', and although they employed artistic licence they probably meant the LT of 1929, which, along with the contemporary ST and the later STL, saw Londoners and millions of servicemen from all over the world through the horrors of World War 2. However, the first of this select band was the B type, which also saw war service, getting on for a thousand being requisitioned during World War 1 to transport soldiers to the Front.

B1 entered service, along with eight companions, on 31 October 1910. By the opening of our decade a 10-year-old bus was ancient indeed, such was the progress in all aspects of the motor vehicle, yet members of the B class were still entering service, and the type did not reach its maximum number, 2,627, until June 1920. Nine years later it had vanished from passenger service.

At Aldgate in 1920 a gaggle of B types mix it with trams of the LCC and East and West Ham corporations. The domed-roof trams were East Ham property dating from 1901/2 and had subsequently been fitted with top covers, which had not exactly added to their rigidity and by 1920 were in a poor state; a number were scrapped and replaced by new cars, whilst the rest were renovated. Tram service 63 was highly intensive but was at a disadvantage in that it was allowed no further than the City of London boundary, whereas the buses could continue right through the City and on into the heart of the West End. *London Transport*

Above: Marylebone Road on a miserable winter's day in 1920. Pursued by a Ford Model T van, a B type on its way to Willesden is passing the 'Yorkshire Stingo' public house, which in 1829 had been the starting-point for Shillibeer's first regular London bus service, to the Bank. A horse-drawn dray is delivering Guinness, Bass and cider as another horse-drawn cart comes plodding along through the wet and slush from the Underground station at the end of the road. *London Transport*

Right: One of the emergency B-type lorry buses, B2496 (LU 8041), repurchased from the War Office in 1919 and pressed into temporary passenger service in 1919/20 to help fill the gap left by other vehicles called up for military service, seen outside Victoria station. If it is on its way to Cricklewood, as the upstairs boards proclaim, then the list of places (affixed to the side) at which it is 'stopping only' makes little sense. But then in the definitive book on the B type, by Robbins and Atkinson (DPR Marketing, 1991) its registration is given as L**H** 8041, so there are two aspects of this picture that don't tie up. *London Transport*

An East Surrey B type, P 8697, *en route* from Ashurst Wood to Reigate, on the edge of the Ashdown Forest, passes Godstone Green in 1920.

Although the vast majority of Bs were double-deck buses, some were single-deckers, and others lorries. Indeed, as was common in early motor-bus days, some of the chassis fulfilled various roles at different times in their careers. The LGOC was desperately short of buses in the immediate aftermath of World War 1, and a few B-type lorries, fitted with longitudinal seats and frames over which a tarpaulin cover could be erected, were pressed into passenger service, running between the summer of 1919 and January 1920. In the early months of 1920 B-type buses that had served in the war were still re-entering service. Known as 'Traffic Emergency Buses', these were a mixed bunch, some being painted red, others khaki, and were not fully up to standard, the former with sub-standard chassis and good bodies brought out of store, the latter with bodies which had been hastily but not fully overhauled. The Metropolitan Police, which exercised rigorous control over the London bus, allowed these vehicles to be licensed for a limited period only, until they could be replaced, and all had gone by the beginning of 1921. However, whilst these 'emergency' buses were being put into service 250 totally new B types were arriving in the fleet, between December 1918 and the spring of 1919. The chassis were brand-new, but whilst this also applied to some of the bodies, the majority had either been completed before the war but not placed on a chassis or been partially finished by the end of 1914, rather like the 'unfrozen' buses of World War 2. It was these, plus the setting up of Chiswick Works in 1921 and its highly efficient overhaul system, which enabled the B type to last until almost the end of the decade.

No sooner had the last new B type entered service (and with refurbished examples still to reappear) than the first of its successors, the K, took up work, in August 1919. The K, whilst still looking old-fashioned by the standards set at the end of the 1920s, was a big step forward from the B. Two features accounted for this. One was the placing of the driver alongside the engine instead of behind it (in other words 'forward' rather than 'normal' control), the other was the rear wheel-arch. Together these features allowed an increase in seating capacity from the 34 of the B to 46 in the K. Putting the driver beside the engine left more room in the lower saloon for passengers, and the rear wheel-arches meant that the entire 7ft 2in width of the body could be utilised — and *that* meant that for the first time transverse seats, two by two either side of the central gangway, could be fitted. In other words the layout with which we are still familiar today had been arrived at.

This was a period of rapid advancement. At an LGOC a board meeting on 15 April 1920 'plans of proposed new types of single-deck and double-deck omnibuses … were considered in detail' by the Directors. It was resolved that 'the plans would be submitted to the Police with a view to obtaining their approval', which was duly obtained, and in December 1920 — a mere 16 months after the first K took up work — its successor, the S type, appeared. Although visually very similar to the K it was longer again, with a small window amidships on either side, between the two long ones. The overlap of no fewer than three generations of LGOC bus is illustrated by a minute of 7 October 1920, wherein it is recorded that orders had been placed for 1,000 K types, 265 Ss and 'seventy-five 26-seater single-deck omnibus bodies to be mounted on "B" type chassis'. On the same date it was noted that 54 B types had been sold for 'about £500 each, a commission of 10% being allowed to Agents'.

It was at this time that the taxation system was changed, and instead of attracting petrol and licence duty each bus with more than 32 seats would be taxed at a rate of £84 per annum. The LGOC estimated that this would cost the company an additional £50,000 each year. Surprisingly, given such a large sum, no comment appears to have been made by the Directors; perhaps any remarks were phrased in such a manner that the scribe taking the minutes could not bring himself to record them in his immaculate, copper-plate handwriting. Partly to make up for this loss, fares were increased by the LGOC and the railways of the Underground Group on 26 September 1920, to one and a half old pennies for two stages of one mile, to two pence for three stages of 1½ miles, and one pence per mile thereafter. Fares thus went up by around 40%. At a meeting of the Board on 7 October the Chairman, Lord Ashfield, and the Managing Director, Frank Pick, recorded that 'every credit was due to all concerned … for the admirable way in which the details [of the increase] had been worked out with a view to causing the least inconvenience to the Public', although it was acknowledged that 'a certain amount of inconvenience was caused to the omnibus passengers desiring to take through journeys which passed through the London County Council Tramway area, thereby necessitating the issuance of several tickets of different denominations'.

The Metropolitan Police now allowed AEC, which produced the chassis, and the LGOC or whoever built the body to produce a bus weighing 8½ tons. Seating capacity went up to 54. Thirty-four years later, when the last RT rolled off the production line,

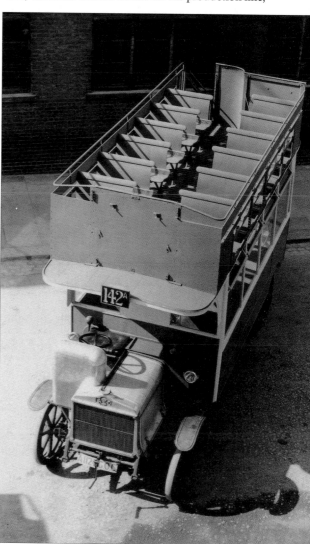

A brand-new K type poses for its picture in August 1920.

Above: Three S types — XH 5956, XH 5929 and XH 5979 — line up with their crews and other officials awaiting the guests for a private excursion from Golders Green c1923. *London Transport*

Below: LE 9830, a 19-seat (note the Hackney Carriage plate at the bottom left hand corner) open charabanc of the LGOC, fitted with pneumatic tyres and photographed in September 1922. *London Transport*

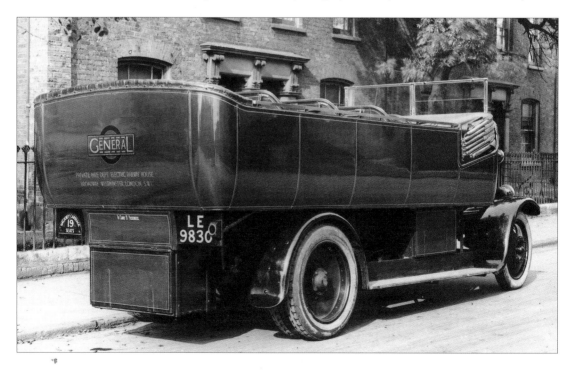

Right: George Shave, Chief Engineer of the LGOC from 1917 to 1933, poses, carnation in button-hole, beside his latest creation, NS1, on 10 May 1923.

A jolly-looking conductor and inspector and a rather more dour driver pose in front of solid-tyred NS1699 of Tottenham garage sometime in the 1920s.

its seating capacity was only two greater, 56 having been the London standard for some 20-odd years. There were 1,132 members of the K class, 928 Ss. A few of each class were fitted with single-deck bodies. Both types had four cylinder petrol engines. The K was rated at 28hp, the S at 35hp. An innovation introduced with the S was the compound volute spring on both axles, which enabled the bus to deal better with variations in weight.

Two and a half years on yet another new type appeared. This was the 35hp NS, the first examples taking up work from Hammersmith garage on route 11 in May 1923. Just exactly what the designation of each London bus type means has for generations been a source of fascination — indeed, of fierce argument leading almost to blows — amongst enthusiasts. Did NS stand for 'nulli secundus' ('second to none')? That would have depended on how many Latin scholars were employed in the Chiswick drawing office. Perhaps it meant 'new S', or maybe 'no step', although strictly speaking this latter was inaccurate, for although it was considerably lower than its

predecessors passengers still had to climb 13 inches from the road to the platform. This involved ladies' showing a fair bit of ankle, something frowned upon when the first Bs appeared, but by 1923 skirt hems were rising rapidly, so there was no longer a problem there. All three suggestions have been put forward, but the most likely (if rather disappointing) explanation is that neither 'NS' nor the type code of any of its successors meant anything very much at all.

Production of the NS continued until 1927, and all were still in service at the beginning of 1930. The highest-numbered example was NS2290, based on a one-off chassis that had been used as an instruction unit at Chiswick before being bodied and placed in service in 1930. Contrasting with previous practice, although Chiswick built some of the NS bodies the majority came from independent builder Short Bros. Over the years various improvements were made to the NS, such that it has been called 'the first modern double-decker', but this term is surely more accurately applied to its successor, the AEC Regent. What is noteworthy is that in October 1925 a batch of NSs — the type having a lower centre of gravity than its predecessors — entered service on route 100 (Elephant & Castle–Epping Town) with covered tops, later to become standard, although some NSs would remain open-top throughout their careers.

In July 1928 the Police allowed pneumatic tyres on the NS, and maximum permitted speed was increased to 20mph. Some NSs had the horizontal-sliding, hurricane-inducing windows, hitherto standard, replaced by vertical wind-down, nice-balmy-breeze-thankyou windows. But many retained their solid tyres, the hardy 'I'll put up with whatever the weather cares to throw at me' drivers having to do without windscreens until 1929 — and even then these were fitted only on an experimental basis. The primitive, minimal front mudguards remained primitive and minimal, route indicators were wooden boards, and route numbers illuminated stencils; the ascent to the upper deck, whether covered or not, was by open staircase, and brackets supporting the lower-deck ceiling were cunningly placed to catch the forehead a nasty wallop as one rose to leave one's seat.

The original NS was actually 3cwt lighter than the S, but the covered-top variety, with upholstered seats upstairs and down, was getting on for a ton heavier. The NS type was the first LGOC bus to have upholstered backs to its lower-saloon seats, wooden backs remaining standard upstairs. In 1926 a new NS with covered top cost around £1,235. One noteworthy variation, which appeared in 1927, was one designed to negotiate the Blackwall Tunnel under the Thames; previously only single-deckers

The bus that never was. Looking like a typical mid-1920s LGOC single-decker, with sliding windows (then very much in vogue), large destination indicator perched somewhat precariously on the roof, pneumatic tyres and standard AEC radiator, R1 was one of a class of five delivered in the summer of 1925. The chassis was designated the 411 (but it may have been a 413); it was also known as the Renown. Of course the far more famous Renown would be the six-wheel double- and single-decker of 1929, but this was a first, for no previous AEC chassis had been distinguished by name. Much good did this do, because, for whatever the reason, R1 was the only one of the five licensed. One authority claims that it never carried any passengers, but the original caption on the back of this photograph states that it was 'used on route 81 Langley–Windsor'. Certainly all five had gone back to the AEC works by the end of July 1925, never to be seen again, although, to quote the late Ken Glazier, 'the bodies were presumably used on five K chassis'. *London Transport*

had been permitted to work through its narrow confines. For the first time a London double-decker had a wholly enclosed upper deck and staircase. Twenty-two (later reduced to 20) deep-cushioned seats, fitted longitudinally, back to back, were provided on the upper deck, and 24 transversely downstairs. The NS 'tunnel buses', as they became known, would be amongst the last of the class to be withdrawn from passenger service, in 1937.

Not quite a dead end, rather a one-off was the massive six-wheel LS of 1927. It had pneumatic tyres, an enclosed upper deck, which extended part way over the driver and bonnet, but an open staircase (originally enclosed), and the driver too was still exposed to the elements. Considered rather sensational on account of its size, it was also the first LGOC bus fitted from new with pneumatic tyres. The class comprised one single-decker and 11 double-deckers. Although the double-deck version originally carried 72 passengers this number was later reduced to 66. Because it was such a revolutionary vehicle just about everyone got involved in its operations from Lord Ashfield, Frank Pick and Ernest Bevin (the trade-union leader and, later, Foreign Secretary in the Attlee Government) to, inevitably, the Metropolitan Police. The 11 LS double-deckers eventually settled down on the 16 group of routes at Cricklewood garage and lasted into LPTB days. *Ian Allan Library*

Above: Oxford Street in 1929. Nearly all the buses, the great majority NSs, have been fitted with top covers and pneumatic tyres. The leading vehicle, dating from 1927/8, is a Guy FCX of City Motor Omnibus Co, with 62-seat Dodson body.

Below: A line-up of Tilling-Stevens Petrol-Electrics in Croydon garage c1925. Tilling-Stevens, of Maidstone, was a big player in the bus business until being almost wiped out by Leyland and AEC at the end of the 1920s; although the firm struggled on in the postwar era it was by then rather like a producer of the occasional black-and-white silent film trying to compete with a Cecil B. De Mille Technicolor spectacular.
Pamlin Prints

· 6 ·

Think of a Number

THE numbering of bus routes is one of those aspects of the London scene which provides endless fascination. Some routes have retained the same number, perhaps with the addition or loss of prefixes or suffixes, since the very earliest days, other numbers disappear and reappear somewhere quite different, whilst in tram days there might be more than one tram route, as well as a bus one, sharing the

No 79, a former LGOC lorry bus fitted with a second-hand B-type body and passed to East Surrey, lays over at the Uckfield terminus of route S9 on 15 January 1923. The S9, running from West Croydon deep into Southdown territory, would later be cut back to Forest Row and renumbered 409.

same number. Indeed, with the reappearance of trams in the Croydon area this is the situation once again. By the early 1920s, particularly with the advent of the unregulated 'pirate' buses, the situation was getting out of hand, and so in 1924 the Metropolitan Police, which controlled so many aspects of public transport in the capital, introduced the London Road Traffic Act — and with it a proper numbering system. Known as the Bassom system, after the acting Chief Constable, this saw central and suburban routes numbered between 1 and 199, those out in the country north of the Thames (which had previously been prefixed with an 'N') between 300 and 399, those south of the Thames (previously prefixed by an 'S') between 400 and 499; numbers in the ranges

Above: The original caption on the reverse of this photograph, dating from 1921, informs us that 'A member of LGOC staff stands in Trafalgar Square talking to the public who are queueing for a bus at an LGOC wooden-style bus stop'. But surely there is a bit more to it than that. The LGOC chap is not pointing in the direction from which any of the 10 pre-Bassom numbers buses listed on the stop are going to arrive, the ladies nearest the camera are not being exactly attentive, instead either chatting amongst themselves or smiling at the photographer, and the bowler-hatted gent looks as if at best he is a very fringe member of the group, hardly more attached than Landseer's lion. In short, the whole thing looks like a bit of a set-up.
London Transport

Right: London General bus map, 1927.

MAP OF THE LONDON
GENERAL BUS ROUTES

Nᵒˢ 5 & 6.   1927.

GENERAL

ISSUED FREE.

LONDON'S
UNDERGROUND

WATERLOW & SONS LIMITED, LONDON, DUNSTABLE & WATFORD

Above: A nasty-looking accident to B592 whilst working the 10B to Epping Town has attracted the inevitable gawping crowd sometime in the 1920s.
Ian Allan Library

Below: A 1926 poster by Dorothy Paton, advertising the delights of LGOC route 81. Dorothy Paton produced a dozen posters for the Underground Group between 1925 and 1929. *London Transport Museum*

East Surrey No 192, an ADC 416A with LGOC bodywork, dating from 1927, on layover at Tunbridge Wells before returning to Horley on route 24. *Pamlin Prints*

200-299 and 500-599 were allocated to routes operated by authorised independents. With the disappearance of the independents the 2xx series became largely the preserve of single-deck routes, and later 500-699 would be reserved for the trolleybuses.

Sometimes it seemed that the Metropolitan Police was too zealous in its regulation of public transport, needlessly holding back progress, but in its defence it could quote examples where it had the good of the travelling public very much at heart. The route-numbering system was one example. Another was its — and successive governments' — concerns over safety.

In 1926, despite the fact that there were fewer than two million vehicles licensed in the UK, there were 4,886 road deaths, which worked out at 2.9 per 1,000 vehicles. Seventy years later, by which time there were nearly 30 million licensed vehicles on our roads, the number of deaths per 1,000 vehicles had dropped to 0.1. At every meeting of the board of directors of the LGOC throughout the 1920s accidents involving buses, fatal or otherwise, were routinely reported. In 1920, for example, LGOC buses were involved in

79 fatal accidents, in 1921 47. The roads of London and its suburbs were dangerous places. Although the LGOC trained its drivers — the famous skidpan at Chiswick being one element of this — no-one had to take a driving test, which did not become compulsory until June 1935, and in 1930, incredible as it may seem, all speed limits were removed, only to be reimposed five years later. Elderly pedestrians attempting to cross the road — there were no marked crossings — were more used to thinking in terms of the top speed of a horse than a motor vehicle, while vehicle brakes, compared with those of today, were highly ineffective and were often fitted only to the rear wheels. In the late 1920s the 6th Earl of Cottenham, a car enthusiast and racing driver, had a radio programme in which he urged motorists to become more skilled; one piece of advice he offered was: 'always be able to stop within the distance you can see to be clear', and he was later recruited by the Metropolitan Police to play a key role at the Police Driving School at Hendon, which did much to monitor and improve road safety.

Above: Working routes which are still to be seen in the West End today, a Metropolitan S and a British NS — the latter with a top cover, but neither yet fitted with pneumatic tyres — await permission to proceed from the imperious figure of the Metropolitan traffic policeman c1927. It is interesting that the S has 'GENERAL' on its radiator, the NS 'AEC'. *London Transport*

Left: YR 3672, an Embassy open-top Dennis fitted with pneumatic tyres and working the 212, heads towards Charing Cross c1929.

Above: One of the curiosities of the Bassom system was that the standard variation of London's most famous route, from Shepherd's Bush to Liverpool Street, was actually numbered the 11A, as seen displayed on the prototype LT1 in 1929.
Ian Allan Library

Left: A three-axle Guy FCX, YT 8954, with Dodson 62-seat body, of Public, dating from 1927. Although the vehicle is fitted with pneumatic tyres and has a covered upper deck, the driver is still without a windscreen. Twelve of these six-wheelers were taken into LPTB custody in 1933/4, this one becoming GS21. All had gone by the end of July 1935.

· 7 ·

The General Strike

THIS began on 3 May 1926. Led by the miners, who were in dire straits, having suffered both wage cuts and an increase in the working day and great unemployment, key workers, such as those involved in transport, were called out throughout the United Kingdom. Labelled revolutionaries by the right-wing press, they received support from a most remarkable source, none other than King George V, who urged: "Try living on their wages before you judge them."

There was some violence, inevitably (although not as much as was claimed by the media), and some of the buses and trams that did run in London, manned by volunteers, were protected by the Police. For example, at the Croydon garage of Thomas Tilling the *Daily Mail* reported 'there was a large gathering of strikers, apparently on a rumour that an attempt would be made to run 'buses by volunteers. A large number of uniformed police were brought to the scene, reinforced by "Specials".' In fairness at least one newspaper, the *Croydon Advertiser*, on 8 May, following dire predictions of imminent anarchy and a proclamation that 'the disruptive effects of the strike are already incalculable', went on to admit that 'in Croydon both the strikers and those hit had displayed exemplary patience and good temper.' Meanwhile, on 7 May, the Trades Union Congress, which was never wholeheartedly behind the strike, met with Sir Herbert Samuel, Chairman of the Royal Commission on the Coal Industry, and as a result the strike was called off on 11 May. All, that is, except for the miners, who managed to stay out until October,

Left: King George V, who would later sympathise with striking workers, in conversation with Lord Ashfield whilst inspecting busmen from Middle Row garage sitting atop 'Ole Bill' at Buckingham Palace, 14 February 1920. *London Transport*

Above: A scene at the LGOC depot in Milman's Street, Chelsea, recoded on 6 May 1926 and featuring an NS surrounded by a group of volunteer drivers who have just passed their driving tests. Clearly the photograph was taken for publicity purposes, for the entire group looks distinctly middle-class, some young enough to be university students, several wearing plus fours.

Left: It's not at all clear exactly what this is, but the likelihood is that it is a lorry, seemingly belonging to one Edward Paul, converted to carry passengers during the General Strike.

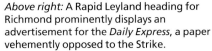

Above: B967 stands at the head of a line of B types, May 1926. A couple of civilian strike-breakers festoon it with barbed wire to frustrate strikers attempting to prevent the bus and its non-union volunteer driver from going about their business. They are watched by a couple of officials, one of whom also seems to be protected by barbed wire, and a soldier standing to attention with fixed bayonet. *London Transport*

Above right: A Rapid Leyland heading for Richmond prominently displays an advertisement for the *Daily Express*, a paper vehemently opposed to the Strike.

Below right: Catford garage during the Strike. A line of Tilling-Stevens Petrol-Electrics is parked outside, beside the tram lines, although, hardly surprisingly, there is no tram in sight. At the head of the line a policeman sits beside the driver of the 36, with chalked 'Marble Arch' destination. Catford garage looks much the same today; buses still park in the forecourt, and although trams no longer run past they can be found a couple of miles away at Beckenham Junction. *The Omnibus Society*

Left: An alternative method of transport to which a few resorted during the Strike was the canal barge, although, of course, these were essentially for goods traffic. This scene, recorded sometime around 1926, is at Uxbridge. It looks supremely rural, but so do sections of the canal network deep in the London suburbs to this day. The boat, probably horse-drawn, is a wide one, 10ft 2in in breadth and therefore not the more common narrow boat. The girl is standing by the beam of the lock gate, whilst her father can just be seen beyond above the tiller, and her mother is standing by the cabin door. The last watermen left the employ of the Underground c1928.

but hardship gradually forced them back to work. Anyone who has ever been down a coal mine could hardly envisage a more appalling workplace, yet when the miners did resume work it was for a longer day, with lower wages and, often, victimisation. The problem was the world demand for coal, which was in decline, but nevertheless the treatment meted out to the miners was scandalous.

One aspect of the strike which still causes some controversy is the 'strike-breaking' by well-educated middle- or even upper-class young men who volunteered to drive buses, trams and trains, man signal-boxes and so forth. For many there was no political motive behind their action – it merely allowed them to realise a boyhood dream. Others felt that they should help alleviate the hardship caused to the general public by the strike, rather ignoring the hardship suffered by the strikers, and particularly their families. At the first meeting of the Board of the Underground Group after the strike, on 20 May, Lord Ashfield praised 'the numerous volunteers and in particular the undergraduates of the Universities of Oxford and Cambridge'. He went on to tell the Board of Directors that he had met union representatives, 'they having called to negotiate a settlement of the strike and to plead for the reinstatement of the Companies' Staff'; they had also 'admitted that they had done the Companies a great wrong in calling the strike and expressed the hope that the future relations with the Companies would be on a much more satisfactory footing'.

· 8 ·

Big Building Projects

UNTIL 1921 the London General Omnibus Co had no central works. When overhaul was due a bus would be driven to LGOC premises — either at Olaf Street, near Latimer Road, or Seagrave Road, in West Brompton — where the body would be removed and attended to, whilst the chassis would be driven back to its home garage and there refurbished. Bodies were built at North Road, Islington, and the chassis and engine, which was almost invariably of AEC manufacture, came from its factory in Blackhorse Lane, Walthamstow. Both the LGOC and AEC were wholly owned by the Underground Group.

It made sense for this vast organisation to set up its own central works where every task could be carried out, and so 32 acres was bought immediately north of

Chiswick High Road, no great distance from the Southall works to which, later in the decade, AEC would move from Walthamstow (which cannot have been a coincidence), and on 8 December 1921 the Board was informed that 'the new Central Overhaul Depot' was 'completely equipped and in full working order'. A jolly was proposed for early the next month, and the Directors would meet at 2.30pm on Thursday 5 January 'for the inspection and the Board Meeting to be held at the conclusion thereof'. With Government backing £5½ million had been allocated for buying the land, building and equipping the works. And 'to relieve unemployment'. Clearly the Directors were pleased, for in February 1923, by which time the works had been operating for some 18 months, they were informed by the Chairman that he had 'received statements showing the benefits which had accrued to the Company as a consequence of the installation of the Works and the transfer of the operations thereto from the Garages which were very satisfactory and which in his opinion merited the congratulations of the Directors'.

Some 3,000 men and women were employed at Chiswick, and the canteen, which also was used for various social activities, dances etc, could seat 1,300. The LGOC was generally a considerate employer and encouraged its employees and their families to take part in various social and sporting activities. At a Board meeting at the end of 1927 authority was given to buy 17 acres, at a cost of £600 per acre, for a sports ground at Bromley; also for the purchase of a piece of land at Kenton and 'the erection of cottage thereon, at cost of £750, to be let to the Groundsman … at 25 shillings per week, excluding lighting and heating'. For the six months ending 30 June that year 'Staff Welfare Expenditure' amounted to £59 14s. In all this Lord Ashfield was a leading light, and the vast London Transport Collection features numerous pictures of the smiling Chairman clearly enjoying himself judging Bonny Baby competitions, awarding prizes on sports days and being an all-round good egg. Frank Pick, a much more retiring personality, seldom features and was no doubt only too happy to let his chairman bask in the limelight.

The LGOC maintained its vehicles to a remarkably high standard and aimed to give each bus a complete overhaul once a year so that it emerged from Chiswick virtually a new vehicle. With nearly all chassis coming from AEC the vast majority of the

Working on an NS. *London Transport*

Left: An aerial view of Chiswick Works.
The main drive from Chiswick High Road leads off to the top left, whilst the test track runs down from the drive towards the bottom of the site, although from this angle it is difficult to see the dip.
District Line tracks are in the foreground.

LGOC's bodies were built at Chiswick, including a few for other operators. Interestingly, tyres were hired, being replaced by the tyre companies' fitters when necessary. A skill presumably not needed at Chiswick was that practised by watermen. In the summer of 1928 it was decided to abolish the 'grade of waterman … the Committee recommend pensions of five shillings per week each to 11 men who had service with the Company prior to employment as watermen'. Sadly we are given no further indication as to what this was all about, and I doubt whether there is anyone surviving who knows the answer. However, a couple of years ago I did have the privilege of interviewing Jack Lemmer, then aged 99, who started out as a trainee engineer at Camberwell garage in 1923 and qualified four years later as a Unit Adjuster (fitter) at Chiswick Works, which, he said, 'simply buzzed with innovative ideas, clever, dedicated men constantly seeking improvements in every aspect of bus design'.

Above: The caption on the back of this official London Underground photograph, taken on 4 May 1929, reads simply 'LGOC garage', but the location is clearly Elmers End, officially opened in March 1929, for construction work is still ongoing around the vehicles. *London Transport*

Below: Elmers End in 1929. This was one of a number of garages which carried out heavy maintenance work, thus allowing Chiswick to concentrate on complete overhauls and new construction. *London Transport*

Charles Holden's drawing of 55 Broadway
— a view from Tothill Street. *London Transport*

The Underground Group had long hankered after a splendid new headquarters in the heart of London. There were various setbacks; for instance in 1920 the first plans were abandoned, architects Richardson and Gill being paid off with a 'reduced fee of 1,500 guineas', the same minute recording that it had been found possible to 'erect a building over St James Park Station (District Railway)'. Thus were taken the first steps towards what has been described as an 'architectural masterpiece', awarded the London Architectural Medal by the Royal Institute of British Architects, but which also led to Pick's offering his resignation — not accepted —

and the removal, so it is alleged, of an inch and a half of the penis of one of Sir Jacob Epstein's sculptures which adorned it. Known simply (and somewhat prosaically) as 55 Broadway, the 10-storey, 175ft-high building — there are a further four storeys in the tower — was at the time of its completion in 1929 the tallest in London. The architect was, it need hardly be said, Charles Holden, who will forever be associated with a succession of wonderful buildings commissioned by the Underground Group and London Transport in the 1920s and '30s. His innate modesty has, like Pick's, made his name less well known than

it might be. It is not too fanciful to claim him as one of the greatest — if not *the* greatest — British architect of the first half of the 20th century.

Constructed of Portland stone fixed to a steel framework, 55 Broadway consists of a central tower from which open-plan offices radiate. Influenced by contemporary American offices, Holden took care with every feature, inside and out, embracing the art-deco style (although this term came in only later). Typically Holden kept the exterior as plain as possible — with one dramatic exception. He commissioned seven leading sculptors, including Jacob Epstein, Henry Moore and Eric Gill, to carve large figures, representing the four winds, directly onto the exterior stonework. It was Epstein's powerful, seemingly primitive and sexually explicit nude figures over the entrances, 'Night' and 'Day', which caused sensitive, conservative souls such anguish, hence the reduction in size of one part of one of the figures' anatomy; further than this neither Pick nor Holden would allow reactionary forces to go. The building has certainly stood the test of time, which has seen the addition a new reception area and a shopping mall (incorporated in the 1980s), and is a listed building, albeit only Grade II — astonishingly, for it stands out like a beacon as a shining example of the very best 20th-century architecture, which London should be proud to celebrate.

The Modern Bus

ONE MAN, G. J. (John) Rackham, was largely responsible for the design of the modern bus, with its powerful, economical engine tucked neatly beside the driver, cranked chassis allowing a lower set body than hitherto and, in the case of the double-decker, seating capacity of around 56. Introduced in the late 1920s, Rackham's Leyland Titan and AEC Regent had almost sole responsibility for removing trams from the streets of the UK, and successive variations on the Regent and Titan theme, including their single-deck Tiger and Regal equivalents, would dominate the British bus and coach scene for some 30 years.

Like a number of other innovative railway and road-transport engineers Rackham had worked on both sides of the Atlantic, as well as being well aware of developments in mainland Europe, and his appointment in 1926 as Leyland's Chief Engineer led to what we may fairly claim was the modern British bus. Having introduced the Titan and Tiger in 1928 he moved on to AEC, and by the end of 1929 the LGOC had placed in service examples of the Regal, plus the six-wheel Renown, the first Regent following early in 1930, although Autocar, of Tunbridge Wells, took delivery in July 1929 of a Regent that would soon become the property of

Left: LT1 entered service towards the end of 1929, the first production batch, comprising LT2-50, being completed in late 1929/early 1930. LT50 is seen in Regent Street, following an NS and overtaking an open-top bus. The original LT design retained an open staircase, which like that of the NS looks very much an afterthought intended for a quite different design of bus; from LT150 the stairs would be enclosed. In most other respects the LT is a great advance on its predecessors. *London Transport*

Above: ST1, with standard LGOC 48-seat body, did not enter service until February 1930, but its design was completed and construction begun in 1929. It wears an experimental livery of red lower panels with cream above, which was not perpetuated, while its fleet number fits awkwardly on the very front edge of the bonnet side; later a standard plate would be fitted. The wide platform and straight staircase represented a huge improvement over the NS class and the first LTs, although the staircase reduced the number of seats. *London Transport*

London General Country Services and, eventually, London Transport ST1139.

The single-deck Regals were placed in the T class, which would feature many variations and be expanded as late as 1948. One of the 1929 buses, T31, survives, beautifully restored to its original condition and can often be seen out and about from its base at Cobham Museum. To quote Alan Townsin, who worked for AEC and is the leading authority on the marque, writing in *Classic Bus* in 2008, 'Much of the mechanical design … was very similar to that of the Leyland Tiger TS1'; he adds that 'Rackham [whom he had met] was aiming at a level of refinement every bit as good as a luxury car', whilst noting: 'the interior of the body seems civilised and well-finished. A remarkably modern feature is the use of translucent ceiling cover panels. The seats

are more comfortable than appearance suggests and, on the move, there is an absence of creaks and rattles. T31 still has the capacity to reach about 50mph.'

Equally advanced were the double-deck LT1 and ST1, although, perhaps inevitably, there remained one or two old-fashioned features: the first 150 LTs had outside staircases, and, in common with the earliest STs, were not allowed windscreens (although eventually the Metropolitan Police relented and allowed these to be fitted retrospectively), while the roller-blind indicators were somewhat restricted in size, and, returning to the driver's lot, no London bus built prior to World War 2 was fitted with a door. However, in terms of passenger comfort no city bus has done much better since, the Chiswick-designed and (in most cases) -built body being a classic which has stood the test of time.

Above: The prototype short-wheelbase AEC Regent, UU 6610 of 1929, in East Surrey livery, poses for its official AEC portrait at Southall. It was also operated by Autocar, of Tunbridge Wells, both companies being part of the LGOC empire. The only General ST with an open-staircase Short Bros body, it would eventually become ST1139. *Ian Allan Library*

Above right: An LGOC Country Services Leyland Lion PLSC, with a 32-seat body built by the LMS Railway at Derby in 1929.

Right: A very rare bird — or rather an AJS Pilot, with Petty 26-seat body, of 1929/30. The bodywork aft of the cab looks perfectly modern, but what a mess the front end is.

Right: A Leyland Titan TD1, with Dodson body, of Glen Omnibus Company in Park Lane on the 73 to King's Cross. It would later become London Transport TD2 and be transferred to the Country Area.

Below: AEC Regal T41. This picture was taken on 9 January 1930, T41 having entered service at the very end of 1929. The Titan and the Regal were both designed by Rackham and were equally modern, yet the simple, classic AEC radiator design put it way ahead of that of contemporary Leylands, whose appearance was rooted in the past. The Lancashire firm would not catch up until 1933.

Above: The immediate predecessor of the Regal was the Reliance 660. The famous AEC triangle is now in evidence, but the almost timelessly simple elegance of the radiator, with its central dividing strip, has yet to be arrived at. This semi-saloon coach of May, 1929 with its part-canvas folding roof, windscreen and neat cab integral with the body (rather than something which still looked as if it should be attached to a horse), was the 'missing link' between the soon-to-be-outmoded designs of the 1920s and the 'modern' bus, represented by the Regal, Regent and Renown.

Right: F. J. Kirk, of Leyton, was one of many independents to buy Regents, VX 7487, of 1929, being an early example. It was fitted with a Dodson body and is seen working the 101 from North Woolwich to Wanstead, which in the mid-1930s was London Transport's busiest bus route.

· 10 ·

Towards the Country and a New Decade

THE 1920s saw wholesale, uncontrolled extension of the London suburbs deep into the countryside, a process that had been proceeding apace since the arrival of the railway. Nowhere was suburbia more rampant than in Metroland. 'Metro-land', as it was originally coined, in 1915, was the area north from Wembley out into the Chilterns,

Above: The Underground had not yet reached this part of Metroland near Amersham when E. Staniland Pugh recorded this scene sometime between 1920 and 1923. Staniland Pugh's fame spread far beyond the Chilterns, yet this was where he mainly worked, one of his most famous images being of two children waving at a Great Central train near Amersham hauled by one of the handsome Robinson-designed 4-6-2Ts. It was titled 'Daddy's Train' — typical of Staniland Pugh's sometimes rather sentimental approach — and appeared in, amongst other publications, *The Wonder Book of Trains*.

served by the Metropolitan Railway. This latter originally had a controlling interest in the Metropolitan Railway Country Estates Ltd, set up in 1919, and although for legal reasons the railway soon gave this up the two worked closely together, which included the railway's nominating the Estates chairman and most of its directors and providing it with offices in the railway's Baker Street headquarters.

Greatly assisted by Poet Laureate John Betjeman, 'Metroland' has entered the language, summarising perfectly the aspiration of the middle and aspiring upper working classes of a house, not rented but bought, on a mortgage, in a leafy suburb where once there were fields — respectable, perhaps, in some eyes, bourgeois and a little dull, the husband most likely working in the City or the West End, reached, of course, conveniently by electric train, the wife using the local bus to go shopping or visit friends and, as a special treat, taking the train once in a while to Baker

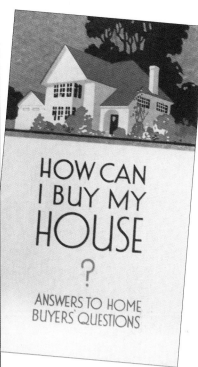

Left: A poster, artist unknown, to celebrate the opening in 1929 of the Chiltern Court restaurant in Baker Street.
London Transport Museum

Above: Useful advice for prospective Metroland residents.

Street to take tea in Chiltern Court, a block of shops and apartments as well as a 250-seat restaurant and a cinema, built above Baker Street station in 1929.

Just as the decade was ending a new method of travelling to the capital from suburbia and beyond was edging its way towards centre stage. In 1928 East Surrey introduced, from Reigate and Redhill to London, express coach services which, although not then successful, pointed the way, and a year later the LGOC inaugurated two routes from Watford, to Golders Green and Charing Cross. Operated by AEC Reliance coaches (the Reliance being the precursor of the Regal), this reprersented the beginning of the Green Line network, officially inaugurated in 1930 and, in modified form, still with us today.

Of course, the irony of all this suburban expansion was that the countryside, such a feature of the publicity, retreated until it had virtually all gone from Middlesex. To quote an advertisement which appeared in *The Railway Magazine* in 1927, 'If you are seeking a home … you will readily find it in Metroland, the glorious countryside, easily and quickly reached by Metropolitan Railway. Nowhere in or around London is there a district that possesses

so many sterling advantages, nor a residential area that so closely approaches the ideal. The train service is frequent and fast, the Season Ticket rates are low, the Educational facilities are excellent and the local Golf courses both numerous and good.' There was obviously also a surplus of capital letters.

Although the Metropolitan Railway had ambitions to extend deep into Buckinghamshire beyond Aylesbury this never really happened, and Great Missenden, some 45-60 minutes' travelling time to Baker Street, is generally accepted as marking the limit of Metroland — although the term was dropped after the Metropolitan Railway had been absorbed by London Transport in 1933. Building nearer London, some of it infilling, some of it over what was left of the countryside, continued apace through the 1930s, coming to a halt only in 1939. After the war, restrictions on ribbon development and establishment of a 'green belt' around London meant an end to the suburban spread.

Elsewhere all around London in the 1920s the suburbs continued to grow, if attracting less media attention than Metroland. The LCC built eight 'cottage-type estates' — 'Homes fit for heroes' — in

locations such as Downham and Poplar, whilst between Barking and Dagenham the Becontree Heath estate, begun in 1921, was the 'biggest in the world'; this was intended partly to re-house people from Poplar, where there was much slum property and considerable unemployment, and by 1932 more than 25,000 'good-quality houses for the better-off working classes but not for the poorer ones' had been built. However, there were complaints that rents were too high, and Becontree was too far away from workplaces, entailing expensive fares by train, bus or tram. The destination 'Becontree Heath', which I used to see on the 25B at Victoria in the 1940s. had for some reason a rather exotic appeal, rather like trams going to 'Beresford Square'; the journey (not that I ever made it) took 106 minutes and cost one shilling and one old penny.

Despite the cost of fares there was considerable migration from the claustrophobic, polluted conditions of the industrialised dockland districts of the East End. Better-off Jews, for instance, from the East End moved out to Dalston, Stoke Newington and Stamford Hill. The 47 tram, which enjoyed a frequency of three to four minutes, took 30 minutes to run from London Docks to Stamford Hill, the fare being 4d, while a trip, on a summer Sunday or bank holiday, from Aldgate out to Epping Forest on LCC tram route 61, operated jointly with Leyton and West Ham corporations, took some 50 minutes and would cost you 6d.

For most Londoners visits to the country meant a train, bus or tram trip. At summer weekends and on

Off for a day in the Surrey countryside on bank holiday in the late 1920s. A large crowd, equipped with raincoats, attaché cases and carrier bags full of comestibles, wait their turn to board an Esher-bound East Surrey bus at West Croydon station. Clearly no one was allowed on an East Surrey bus unless sporting a hat, and even if it was bank holiday male passengers were expected to wear a tie. The gantries supporting the overhead power lines of the LBSCR electrification, soon to be swept away and replaced by the Southern Railway's third rail, are still in place. The Marie Lloyd appearing at the Penge Empire was the daughter of *the* Marie Lloyd, who had died in 1922, but was a successful star in her own right if not as original as Harry Tate, a wonderfully funny Scottish comedian celebrated for his motoring sketch. He would die from injuries suffered in the Blitz.

bank holidays bus services reached far out from Central London, and much patience was required, for families might queue for hours before finding a place and then be bounced around for up to two hours on the top deck of a solid-tyred bone-rattler (all right on a nice day, but fine weekend and bank-holiday weather was no more guaranteed then than it is now). The experiences of a Croydon man at Easter 1926 as quoted in the *Croydon Times* are worthy of note: 'May I point out that the people who could not get on the East Surrey 'buses last Easter Monday were comparatively fortunate, for those who did get a seat and were conveyed to Coulsdon Common or Upper Caterham found themselves stranded when

S186 (XH 3386) on layover in a rather damp Trafalgar Square whilst the driver puffs away on his pipe before setting off for the outer-suburban-cum-rural delights of Belmont and Epsom. The chance of winning £5 a week for life would have tempted many a working man in the mid-1920s.

night came. Dozens of people waited for two hours on the Surrey hills trying to get back to Croydon, but the cry was "Sorry! Full up! No standing allowed!" Some set off to Caterham Railway Station, others made for Coulsdon Station with sleeping children in their arms. Coming down to Purley at half-past nine we found no crowd, in fact the London County Council [tram] cars were leaving comparatively empty. I think we may come to the conclusion that where we have trams, LGOC 'buses and independent 'buses catering for the traffic the people can travel even at busy times, but where on a semi-country service one company has the monopoly the people of Croydon, especially those with young children, would do well at holiday times or on fine Sundays to think twice before they render themselves liable to a journey of perhaps four miles to a railway station.'

Yet since the end of the Great War events had been conspiring to bring about the amalgamation of all public-transport providers in London and its suburbs. In the summer of 1920 Lord Ashfield and the Minister of Transport had agreed upon 'the necessity for the unified operation of local passenger transport services in London and adjacent districts', and in 1924 a somewhat watered-down bill passed through Parliament, resulting in the formation on 1 September of that year of the London & Home Counties Traffic Advisory Committee. Taking advice from Frank Pick, the committee in the summer of 1927 issued a report which recommended the setting up of a unified body to run public transport in the capital. In June 1929 a Labour Government took power, Herbert Morrison (later to become leader of the London County Council and eventually, in the Attlee Government of 1945, Deputy Prime Minister), becoming Minister of Transport, and from then there followed an inexorable progression towards the establishment on 1 July 1933 of the London Passenger Transport Board.

Left: A rural scene from April 1923 which is not what quite what it appears to be, for it features a line of B-type buses and at least one charabanc that have conveyed spectators to the 1923 Cup Final at Wembley and are parked nearby whilst the match is in progress. Wembley was then on the very edge of the countryside, in Metroland.
London Transport

Right: Ransomes-bodied PS140, still running on solid tyres, stands in front of Godstone garage before setting off for West Croydon on the 409. The suit belonging to the smiling chap leaning on the offside front mudguard looks less than immaculate; is he a mechanic? PS140 had entered service in 1924 and would be withdrawn in 1931. *Alan B. Cross / G. Robbins collection*

Left: PS126, an example of the London General Country Services version of the S, stands at the Bromley North terminus of the 410 route *c*1929. Allocated to Reigate garage, the PSs would be replaced in 1934 by lowbridge provincial-style STLs. Whilst working on this book the author interviewed Stanley, an amazing 94-year-old former employee of the London General Country Services who had worked at Reigate garage in the 1920s and who did his courting on the open top deck of a PS.

Right: McKnight Kauffer's 1920 poster extolling the delights of St Albans. The 84 would have taken you all the way there from Golders Green. Edward McKnight Kauffer was very nearly the most important graphic artist of the period. Born in the USA in 1890, he visited Germany and France in 1913, took in all that was going on in the *avant-garde* art world and settled in England, where almost immediately he was commissioned by Frank Pick to design posters for the Underground. He attempted to join the British army but as an American citizen was rejected. He and Pick were kindred spirits, Kauffer writing that he 'could see no reason for conflict between good art work and good salesmanship'. A painter and film-maker, he became the supreme graphic designer, completely at ease with business leaders yet never compromising on his æsthetic instincts. Afforded the rare accolade of a one-man show at the Museum of Modern Art in New York, he later returned to that city and died there in 1954.
London Transport Museum

Above: The caption on the back of this photograph of an LGOC 32-seater 95hp Reliance motor coach delivered in May 1929 draws our attention to the 'special screen … fitted at far end of coach to prevent back draught'. The centre section of the roof could be opened, hence the clips attached to the struts. *London Transport*

Below: A coach party in an open charabanc belonging to one of the many independents eventually absorbed by the LGOC and the LPTB, about to set off for a tour of the Chiltern autumn colours, 1 October 1928.

A BARTHOLOMEW/LONDON TRANSPORT SOUVENIR MAP

LONDON 1928

Country Bus Routes

COLLECTORS' SERIES

Left:
Country Bus Routes map, 1928.

Below:
Camden Town, February 1921. It may be the depths of winter, but there is no shortage of customers eager to sample an open-top ride on a solid-tyred B type to Reigate, with plenty more queuing on both sides of the road. They bred 'em tough in those days. *London Transport*

Right: Passengers queue at Charing Cross on Whit Monday (19 May) 1924 to board the 119 to Chislehurst.
London Transport

Below: 'Ho for the open road.' Hats firmly in place, two London General charabanc-loads of hardy excursionists head out into the Chilterns on what looks like a not particularly sunny 6 May 1924.
London Transport

Above: The year 1929 marked the centenary of London's buses, and the LGOC went to town on the celebrations, including this splendid replica of Shillibeer's original three-horse bus, seen galloping along Cheapside. *Pamlin Prints*

Left: A picture taken — on the occasion of the 1929 centenary of London's first Shillibeer omnibus — of the driver and conductor of preserved B type 'Ole Bill'. The LGOC driver, wearing his contemporary summer-issue white dustcoat — and medals — looks quite at home posing for his official portrait, whilst alongside him his lady conductor, dressed in the uniform of the 1914-18 period, looks rather less at ease. *London Transport*

Bibliography

A History of the Metropolitan Railway Vol One,
Bill Simpson, Lamplight Publications, 2003

Underground Movement, Paul Moss, Capital Transport,
2000

The Metropolitan Railway, C. Baker, Oakwood Press,
1951

The Battles of the General, Ken Glazier, Capital
Transport, 2003

The London B Type Motor Omnibus, G. J. Robbins
and J. B. Atkinson, World of Transport, 1991

Chiswick Works, Colin Curtis and Alan Townsin,
Capital Transport, 2000

London Independent Bus Operators 1922-1933,
D. E. Brewster, Oakwood Press, 1972

The Metropolitan Electric Tramways Vol 2 1921-33,
C. S. Smeaton, The Light Rail Transit Association,
1986

General Buses of the Twenties, George Robbins,
Images Publishing (Malvern) Ltd, 1996

London's Underground Suburbs, Dennis Edwards,
Capital Transport, second edition 2003

Bright Underground Spaces, David Lawrence,
Capital Transport, 2008

Steam to Silver, J. Graeme Bruce, Capital Transport,
revised edition 1983

London Bus File 1933-39 (Double-deckers), Ken Glazier,
Capital Transport, 2001

London Bus File 1933-39 (Single-deckers), Ken Glazier,
Capital Transport, 2002

Tramways of Croydon, G. E. Baddeley, The Light Rail
Transit Association, 1983

Steam on the Underground, Martin Smith, Ian Allan, 1994

London Transport Bus Garages, John Aldridge, Ian Allan,
2001

London Tramways, John Reed, Capital Transport, 1997

London Transport Tramways 1933-1952, E. R. Oakley and
C. E. Holland, London Tramways History Group,
1999

London Route Review 1934-39, LOTS, 1991

Pleasure Trips, Jonathan Riddell, Capital Transport, 1998

Various company documents in the London Transport
Museum and London Metropolitan Archives.

Minutes of the Directors of the London General
Omnibus Company

Croydon Times

Little and large Lacre three-wheel sweepers.
There were originally 41 of these curious machines,
dating from the 1920s, which were used at Chiswick
Works and in garages and were therefore never
registered. Fitted with solid tyres, one of the large
versions survived well into the 1950s. The back of
the photograph is marked 'experimental', which
presumably refers to the vehicle on the right,
for the other is a standard design.
Ian Allan Library